I Miss
My Dad…

Eric Tomei

Flagstone Circle Publishing

I Miss My Dad…
Copyright © 2008 Eric Tomei
Published by Flagstone Circle Publishing

All rights reserved. No part of this book may be reproduced (except for inclusion in reviews), disseminated or utilized in any form or by any means, electronic or mechanical, including photocopying, recording, or in any information storage and retrieval system, or the Internet/World Wide Web without written permission from the author or publisher.

For further information:
eatomei@comcast.net

Printed in the United States of America

I Miss My Dad…
Eric Tomei
1. Title 2. Author 3. Inspirational

Library of Congress Control Number: 2008900684

ISBN 10: 0-9815143-0-8
ISBN 13: 978-0-9815143-0-7

You are about to read about an ordinary man who lived an extraordinary life. Thank you for sharing this tribute to a great man, my Dad. I hope that you will know him as well as I do.

15% of each sale from every book will be donated to Habitat for Humanity, my Dad's favorite charity. Thank you for taking time to read this and for supporting a great charity. Please visit their website at: www.habitat.org to learn how you can volunteer your help.

Dedicated to all sons and daughters who have lost their Dad or loved one

TABLE OF CONTENTS

FOREWORD ix

"A LETTER TO DAD" xiii

CHAPTER 1: Days 1

CHAPTER 2: Tasks 5

CHAPTER 3: Advice 15

CHAPTER 4: Humor 24

CHAPTER 5: Sports 30

CHAPTER 6: All Those Little Things 37

CHAPTER 7: Knowing Him Today 54

CHAPTER 8: Vacation of a Lifetime 57

CONCLUSION 71

ACKNOWLEDGEMENTS 73

FOREWORD

It was 11:50 AM on January 29, 2006, when the phone rang. I was working on the computer in the spare room in my house when I saw it was my sister. I almost let the call go to voice mail, as I sometimes do, when I am working on something important. That Sunday morning, though, something told me to pick up the phone. Little did I know that my life would never be the same.

I said hello to my sister in the most cheerful way possible. She blurted out, "Something has happened to Dad." I thought I knew better. Nothing happens to my Dad. He never gets sick, not even a cold. I asked her what was wrong. She told me to "Drive to St. Mary's hospital." Then I hung up. At that point I knew he was dead.

I had exactly one hour of driving time to think about how to best prepare myself for this life changing event. When I got to the hospital, my Mom was with him holding his hand and there were no monitors hooked up. There were signs of neither the life nor the vitality he regularly exhibited.

It was later explained that he was sitting on the bed getting ready for church and, turning to answer a question my Mom had asked, he fell face first into the bedroom wall. My Mom yelled for my sister to come to the room while she called 911. My sister courageously tried to perform CPR until the paramedics arrived, but he was already turning blue. Their efforts were nothing short of miraculous in a horrific situation.

No warning, no time to prepare, no time to say goodbye. Ten seconds can permanently transform so many lives. It was like walking through your worst nightmare yet everything happened in real time. Nothing made sense, but it was the reality you were forced to accept. From that day forward, life took on a much different perspective. Piece by piece, we had to begin putting a puzzle together that we did not have a picture for.

I remember arriving home with my Mom and sister and just looking around the room, not at each other, but realizing that the morning was so much different than that afternoon. Everyone, including myself, was so overcome with emotion that the only thing I knew to do was to start planning and organizing things, just like Dad would have done. There were plenty of things to do and I needed to complete each of them in order to cope with the situation. It was my way of dealing with the magnitude of it all.

My first few fatherless days were spent contacting family, friends, lawyers, financial planners, business partners, co-workers past and present, making funeral home arrangements, and picking cemetery plots. It was the most horribly unfair situation, I thought, ever to be put in. Our family had to deal with all of this at once. Not to mention the fact that my Dad just died. The breadwinner had passed. Bills needed to be paid. So many thoughts were running through our heads, we did not know what to focus on first. And let me tell you that until you have picked out cemetery plots with your one remaining parent, it is hard to understand the reality of how death truly affects a family.

When my Dad died it was the biggest shock to our whole family. Thank God we have a strong family, but even the strongest of families can have their patience and resolve tested. But that is the power of family, a power that should never be underestimated, especially in times of peril. Death can either divide a family further or unify a family stronger than it has ever been before. We had to wait four months to find out the cause of death. His diagnosis: a "heart attack, due to advanced cardiovascular disease."

My Dad was the picture of perfect health: 6 feet tall, 170 pounds, never been in a hospital in his life. He was not even born in a hospital; he was born in a barn in Italy! He looked healthy. What we found out is that my Dad really started dying 20-25 years ago, he just did not know it, and, for that matter, neither did his family.

This is why heart disease is commonly referred to as the "silent killer." He went for regular physicals and passed all EKG tests. All the common risk factors for heart disease such as high blood pressure, diabetes, smoking, high cholesterol, and family history were absent. We were simply left to wonder, what in the hell just happened? However, my Dad also had a desk job for most of his life, never exercised, and had irregular eating habits. The point being that if you suspect your loved one has risk factors for cardiovascular disease, please have him or her checked by your family physician. It may make the difference between whether you pay a bill for a doctor or a funeral.

It is never too late to save someone you love or care about. It is too late for my Dad, but it does not have to be so for yours. Make him listen. His life depends on it. And for all the Dads out there reading this book, do not make your lasting legacy to your children one of stubbornness and pride. It is perfectly acceptable to go to the doctor and get regular checkups. It is all right to go see a specialist for a problem that requires further attention. Do not rob yourself of a lifetime of memories with your loved ones because you want to "tough it out."

Please refer to the American Heart Association's website for further information regarding how to help your loved one. Don't wait.

www.americanheartassociation.org

"A LETTER TO DAD"

Dear Dad:

    At times, it seems like you have been gone forever and at times it seems just like yesterday. When you left, you made me a member of a club I never wanted to be a part of. On January 29, 2006, I officially became a member of the Lost Dad's Club.

    So much change has happened since you left us and, yet, so many things remain the same. Life as we know it has been changed forever and at times it seems impossible to move forward. You have cast such a powerful shadow on the people that love and care for you that your legacy stretches deeper and wider then you will ever know. The relationship that we had has left a permanent imprint on everything that I do.

    Often times, I feel like our relationship has grown stronger even though I cannot see you. I find myself talking to you about nothing in particular, but then again, we always talked about nothing in particular. In every situation in life I have encountered since you left us, I always ask myself the question, "What would Dad do in this situation?" Then I realize the real question I should be asking myself is, "What would Eric do in this situation?" You have taught me the importance of the power of choice, among many other things.

    They say an academic education is life's greatest learning experience. I respectfully disagree. The education about life that YOU taught me was my greatest learning experience. You taught me to be calm amidst the chaos, confident in the wake of fear, definite in times of indecision, and most importantly, how to be a friend amongst enemies. You have taught me that experience is truly the best teacher and to embrace equally both success and failure.

    There are plenty of both in life and important lessons from these can be learned and applied with an open mind and heart. You opened my eyes to the fact that success is something to be achieved every single day, for that is all we are given. You have taught me that the true measure of success is the excellence with which you live your life. Most importantly, you impressed upon me the importance of not only being a good son but also a great man. I hope you know how grateful I am for the lessons you have taught me about this crazy journey called life.

I want to thank you, Dad, from the bottom of my heart. Thank you for all the good times and the bad. It has been a fantastic ride and if I had to do it all over again I would not change a thing. I only hope I can follow in the giant footsteps you have left behind.

But then again, you would never want me to follow in your footsteps, but rather create my own path for future generations. Because of you, I embrace the fact that everyone must follow their own path too. Hopefully, we will one day meet in the same place.

This book is my lasting tribute to you. Thirty years of the good, the bad, and everything in between. Thank you, Dad, for letting me share in this journey with you. Thank you for teaching me that an ordinary person can also lead an extraordinary life. We will meet again someday, but that doesn't mean that the struggles of life are any easier without you. No matter how long I live, it will be hard not to miss you.

My deepest admiration and respect,
—Eric

CHAPTER 1
Days

"It is not how much we have, but how much we enjoy, that makes happiness."
—Charles H. Spurgeon

As most of you know, special days of the year such as holidays and birthdays can bring up bittersweet memories of the time spent with your Dad or other loved ones. For some, remembrance of these special occasions causes pain and grief, whereas others cannot help but to smile at past events. It is no different for me and my family. While I am a big birthday guy, my Dad was not. As a result, his birthday for me is a sad occasion because he is no longer here to celebrate it.

However, he never liked celebrating it when he was here. Each individual will have their special "day" that they remember Dad, and it certainly does not have to be any set day. It is important, however, to take the time to reflect on the special occasions you had with your Dad and what you gained from those experiences.

I miss my Dad because…

❖ the last time we were out in public together was January 7, 2006, at my brother-in-law's 30th surprise birthday party. It was three weeks before my Dad's death. He bought me three beers. I thought it was cool especially since I could afford the beers myself. I should have known something was up.

* on Sunday, January 8, 2006, we were changing a tire together. I had a slow leak in my back tire and my Dad offered his assistance to fix it. We patched and changed that tire in about 30 minutes. There were no arguments, disagreements, or fights. We worked as a team to get the job done. As I was leaving to go home, I remember my Dad doing something he had NEVER done before. He stood outside the garage and waved goodbye to me. Little did I know that would be the last time I would ever see him alive.

* he gave my Mom a Valentine's Day card every year.

* he never cared about his own birthday. His famous line was, "It's just another day."

* I think about how little he cared about his birthday. I am a big birthday guy and I would steal his planner at the beginning of the year and make sure that he knew when my birthday was. I used to write it in big capital letters. I do not think he ever found that funny.

* on his birthday I established the tradition that I will go to his favorite restaurants and order what he would. Buying Little Caesars Pizza with ham, green pepper, and light sauce was one of his favorites.

* one year I got him exactly what he wanted for his birthday: nothing. He seemed genuinely happier that I got him nothing rather than something.

* he dyed Easter eggs with us every year and seemed to enjoy it.

* he made one of the smartest decisions of his life on May 31st, 1969: The day he married my Mom.

* he won't have a chance to pretend to like the gifts I bought him on Father's Day. This day still stings. It is a reminder that you have something missing from your life that most people at your age do not. My Dad was generally less appreciative of gifts that we got him, but it was still his day. I miss not being able to give him a Home Depot gift card. Father's Day, by far, is the hardest day of the year.

* every Father's Day at our church they used to reward the oldest Dad, the newest Dad, the Dad with the most teenagers, and the Dad with the most kids, with a plant. One year, my Dad actually won for…the most teenagers. My sisters and I were laughing. I really do

not remember what happened to that plant, but at least he walked out of church with a gift.

* the tie I got him for Father's Day in 1987, he finally wore in 1997.
* my Dad, both Grandpas, and myself celebrated my 21st birthday at the Knights of Columbus. I was drunk in the middle of the day. I remember all of my Grandpa's friends were so nice because they brought me beer after beer. Being a college student at the time, I loved it. The ladies of the family never found out how much I had to drink that day.
* he always took us trick-or-treating every Halloween.
* he could carve Bert and Ernie from Sesame Street into a pumpkin without a template. I was convinced that they did not look anything like them until the first kid came to the door for candy and said, "Hey, Bert and Ernie." My Dad was smiling. He was the master pumpkin carver.
* he helped carve the turkey at Thanksgiving.
* he hated hanging up Christmas lights.
* one year for Christmas when I was six, Santa Claus came to our house and brought us presents and told us stories. I really thought that was cool. Of course I did find out later that my Dad hired someone from work to play Santa and give us gifts, which I thought was even better.
* every Christmas he would tell us a story about how he got an orange for Christmas in Italy every year when he was a kid. Can you imagine any kid getting an orange for Christmas now?
* one year I thought I was going to catch my Dad stuffing gifts in the stockings so I snuck down and waited by the stairs. I naturally got bored with all of the waiting because I was little and he could stay up much later than me. I fell asleep on the stairwell and my Dad woke me up to go to bed. After that, the Santa adventure was over.
* when I was eight he asked me when my Mom's birthday was. He thought it was Dec. 5th. I politely reminded him that it was Dec. 7th.
* holidays take on a different meaning. New traditions are being established and old memories are cherished.
* he got up at 5AM with my Mom to help put the turkey in the oven for Thanksgiving. It was an annual ritual that they both looked forward to.

* because new family traditions are continually being created without him.

* he saved all birthday, Father's day, and anniversary cards in a shoebox which I found on a shelf in his bedroom.

* his morning time was the most important time of day.

* I am saddened that he will not get a chance to walk my other sister down the aisle at her wedding.

CHAPTER 2
Tasks

"Do the hard jobs first. The easy jobs will take care of themselves."

—*Dale Carnegie*

It seems like everyone's Dad is good at something. Whether it is a task like keeping finances, handyman work, outdoor landscaping, painting or design, and other skills, it will be unique to the relationship. Every Dad is good at something, but my Dad was good at every single one of these tasks. There was nothing he could not fix. He always seemed to know the answer to a situation, even when he did not. I believe he tried to instill that genius in me. No matter what the situation or problem, he found that there was always a solution. The solution may not readily come to you, but it is always there. It is your job to analyze and propose the best action to ensure success in any of life's "little situations" that you are confronted with.

One thing my Dad was known for was by starting a task, be prepared to finish that task to the best of your ability. Plan on devoting 100% of your time and efforts to make sure the job is done right. Hard work, dedication, and perseverance in any task ensures success. I have used this advice from my Dad numerous times in my life and I can honestly tell you it has never let me down.

I miss my Dad because…

* I enjoyed watching him interact with his Dad. It was entertaining to watch him be the son for a change.
* he never let me cut the grass. I think the last time I cut it I was 10. I never cut the grass "just right" according to him so he never wanted me to cut it again. Being 10 years old, I thought it was awesome. I mean, who really wants to cut the grass?
* he constantly adjusted the thermostat in the house. It really never was the right temperature no matter what time of the year it was. He always had a bad habit of adjusting the thermostat in my house when he came over. So one time I taped the dial shut so he could not adjust it and would have to take the tape off if he wanted to. You know, that day, I never saw him go near that thermostat.
* of his devotion and practice of strict religious principles which were the guiding forces in his life.
* one of the best childhood memories I have with my Dad is when we were in the "Father/Son Bake-off" in Cub Scouts when I was eight. The rule was that Moms could not help in baking cakes. I thought, even then, we would lose because the only thing my Dad knew how to make was scrambled eggs and sausage. To make matters worse, the theme of the bake-off was television shows and games. The odds were not in our favor because my Dad hated playing games and the only TV show he watched was the news. We played **Chutes and Ladders** one day and my Dad said, "We should make this into a cake." I definitely agreed with this great idea. After all, it was one of my favorite games growing up. The cake turned out awesome. It was a yellow cake with white icing and gumdrops for the board markers. I remember using pieces of red licorice for the chutes and toothpicks for the ladders. I remember my Dad asking me why we did not make the cake chocolate. I said, "I don't like chocolate and I want to be able to eat a piece after we're done." We took third place and it was a lot of fun. My Dad took a picture of the cake, which I still have today, but I cannot remember if either of us ever enjoyed a piece of that **Chutes and Ladders** cake.
* he could make a great Pinewood Derby car. For anybody not into Cub Scouts or Boy Scouts, the Pinewood Derby is an annual car race where you basically have to construct a car out of a block of

wood, some nails, sandpaper, and not much else. The cars would race and prizes were awarded to the fastest car. The first year we entered the Pinewood Derby race I was seven. It was held in my elementary school gym. Back then, I cared less about the car, but more about winning that race. So my Dad and I set up shop in the basement on the little green card table we had and we went to work on it for approximately three weeks. I went through the process with my Dad because he was the boss and knew more about this than I did. Honestly, I would have rather been playing outside. We painted the car metallic blue with flame decals on each side of the car. It was sleek and sporty as much as a Pinewood Derby car could be. I was #26. The car looked awesome. We ended up with a gold medal which gave me playground bragging rights for the rest of that week. We did not win the entire event, but our car ranked in the top five. I walked out of that gym that night smiling ear to ear. That was such a fun experience which I looked forward to every year.

* he used to stop at green lights and my Mom would yell at him for doing it. In his mind, I was the bad driver.

* he used to clang the spoon against the bowl when eating ice cream. I remember turning up the volume on the TV to drown out the noise he was making with the spoon. Then he would yell because the TV was too loud. Looking back on it, I should have found more patience, or at least had a bowl of ice cream and clanged my spoon louder.

* I got in trouble for walking out in the street in front of a car to get a soccer ball right in front of him. I was nine and that car had to slam on the brakes so hard, I think it created a fire. I ran away from the house because he was really mad. When I returned, I got in trouble for both running in front of the car AND for running away from the house.

* he was the first person in his family to go to college, and I am proudly the first person in my family to graduate from college. Dad paved the way again.

* he took so much time researching our family roots. He spent hours on the computer making flow charts and doing research. He actually bought a software program to make the flow charts. He had a station in the basement where he would collect pictures of old relatives. Those pictures told so many stories about the quality of the

relationships in our family. It was truly his pride and joy, and with good reason.

* he helped me build a bridge for a contest in Physics class in high school. This activity was exciting to him because it had a lot of engineering principles in it and he was a great engineer. I needed his help really bad. I was getting a C in Physics class and the final exam was coming up. That was not a great position to be in. The winner of the bridge building contest, though, would receive forty extra credit points toward the final exam. My Dad and his friend at work helped me out tremendously. When he started talking about forces, vectors, and lever arms, I got lost. He might as well have been speaking a foreign language. I honestly couldn't have been more bored with the project, but it was a good bonding experience for the both of us. I ended up finishing second and my Dad helped me from failing the final exam. A weighted bucket of sand was the measure for how strong the bridge was. After explaining to my Dad that this how the project would be scored, he told me, "Whatever you do, don't have them put that weighted bucket in the middle of the bridge because that's the weakest point on the bridge." When he asked me why I received second place, I told him it was because I let them put the weighted bucket of sand in the middle. It was in the heat of the competition and I told my Dad I just was not thinking. My Dad was not happy but he said, "Second place is better than last." The joke between us from that point on was that every time we did something that was not the best choice, we would say "put the weight in the middle." Nobody else understood what we were talking about, but that is why it was one of our inside jokes. He saved that bridge and always displayed it on his desk at work.

* we would get up at 5:30AM with my uncle and cousins to set up for the annual family picnic. Everybody was yelling and swearing while we moved picnic tables and cleaned up the campsite, and when the picnic started, we all got along just fine.

* he taught me to NEVER waste food, and I really took that to heart as I became an adult. He always taught us the value and importance of a meal. We volunteered as a family for various food charities and soup kitchens over the years. My Dad wanted us to see that not everybody can go into the refrigerator and get what they

want, when they want it. One time we went to St. Pat's Soup Kitchen in downtown Detroit with our church and I worked my butt off cleaning tables, serving meals, and talking with people. I think we were down there four hours and I do not remember even talking with my Dad while we were there. That experience always had a lasting impact on me. Somewhere, somebody does not have enough to eat so I always appreciate the value of a good meal.

* I will never forget the look of happiness on his face when he walked my sister down the aisle at her wedding.

* he was the worst singer at church. He sounded like me when I went through puberty. I always had to pretend I was laughing at something else in church. Being Catholic, you are not expected to laugh at most things in church. But it was so funny. And, yet, he sang.

* he used to work at home from 10PM-1AM. Then, he got up at 5AM and worked some more. This went on for 30 years.

* on his suggestion, our family served Christmas dinner to those who were less fortunate than us at a local soup kitchen. It was an experience that each of us still fondly remembers.

* he would build a fire in the fireplace. We actually had a brick fireplace with a brick chimney. Chopped firewood laid nearby on a cement porch that he built next to the house. I have many fond memories of cold winter nights and that warming fire.

* he bought me my first car in 1993. It was a 1986 gray Pontiac Sunbird. The car is difficult to find anymore, but the jokes my friends and I had about that car were classic.

* I never once heard him complain about decisions he made in his life. I did however hear him loudly complain about the decisions I made at times.

* he had the courage to start his own company in 1985. He also had a wife and three kids to support while doing so.

* he went to a doctor's appointment with me one time for an infection I had as a result of that surgery. I warned him exactly what they were going to do. They had to cauterize a wound that was below my lower back with silver nitrate and it burned like hell. I did not think he believed me, so I took him with me to the appointment. I asked for a towel to bite on, which I always did, before the procedure took place. My Dad was right there and witnessed the whole thing:

my getting burned by the silver nitrate, my biting the towel, and never flinching. On the car ride home, he had nothing to say to me. It was the only time that I remember he did not have anything to say.

* the only picture in his office when my sister and I went to go clean it out after he died was one of him and me at my high school graduation party.

* he loved Habitat for Humanity. When he retired, a family joke because we knew he never was going to, he always talked about volunteering to build houses all day. This would have, for him, defined happiness.

* when I was going to college, he bought me a book of the best colleges and universities in the United States. He gave me this book, easily 500 pages thick, and wanted me to pick the best in Michigan, my home state.

* he told me one time how much money he made at his job. I thought that was such a big deal because he was such a private person. That showed a lot of trust and confidence on his part.

* it was the BIGGEST deal when we moved anything in or out of the house. An example I remember clearly was that we were moving a pool table into my Grandma's basement. It was one of these old fashioned pool tables with cherry wood and a slate felted top. This pool table was so big that we had to take it apart in sections to take it down the basement. It took six people to move the slate top of the pool table. That top was the heaviest thing I have ever lifted. My Dad decided he was going to be in charge of directing this pool table down the stairs and into the basement. It was a debacle from the start. I tripped going into the house with the slate top and it really is not a good idea to trip when you are carrying heavy slate with five other guys. As we proceeded to go down the stairs, the pool table did not fit. We were literally stuck with this pool table standing straight up on the stairs and nowhere to go. I just started to laugh. I thought it was hilarious. My Dad on the other hand did not. He started yelling at me to stop laughing while the pool table was stuck. So I said, "You're right, laughing at the pool table being stuck is not going to help matters, yelling at it definitely will." I am glad we were on opposite sides of the pool table that day.

* he liked to sit out on our front porch during a violent rainstorm. He loved watching lightning.

* he never trusted me around an open flame whether it was on the stove, grill, or while getting gas for the lawn mower. I guess that was probably a good thing.
* he really did love animals even though he said he wasn't an animal lover. We bought a dog, as a gift, for my aunt on her 80th birthday. It was a surprise so my Mom and Dad picked up the dog the week before the party. My Dad made a little bed for it and took care of the dog until the party. He really showed the soft spot in his heart for animals.
* he used to hate painting walls. It was the one household job he hated to do, but he hated it even more to have to pay someone else to do it.
* he believed in the power of recycling in order to make the world a better place.
* he marked all of the children's heights on a 2 X 4 piece of wood in the garage. It was labeled with the first letter of your name and your age at the time of the measurement.
* when I was younger and we would get dressed up to go to a family event, he always shined my dress shoes. He had every color shoe polish in an old wooden case that had a spot where you could put your shoe on the top of it. It was located in the basement by the washer and dryer. I remember really loving the smell of the shoe polish and how impressed I was that my shoes shined after that. You knew it was a special occasion when you got your shoes polished.
* he knew how much I liked to play basketball as a kid so he built a backboard for me and got an old basketball hoop from my cousins. He did not want to spend money for a store-bought backboard and hoop.
* he was always working on some sort of project: home improvements, yard work, tracing the family tree, or researching investments.
* he told my Mom to call me to see how I was doing. He, however, was not a phone person.
* he tried to give me money after coming home for the weekend from college. It was his way of saying "I love you" without actually having to say it. But I never took the money. Looking back though, I should have, I was a poor college student and he owned his own company.
* he rarely had the patience to explain things to me. He always

felt like I should know the answer to everything. What he never realized, however, was that I did not care if he did not know the answer to something. I cared that he tried to find the answer out.

• we did projects together. I remember one time we were painting some walls in my condo. We listened to smooth jazz for 6-8 hours. If you can survive listening to music that you hear on most of America's elevators, then you can survive just about anything. I prefer rock and roll.

• he used to show us old home movies when we were younger. He had this projector that looked like it was fresh out of the 1950's. It made that whirring sound when you turned the machine on. There was also an old, ripped projector screen that he used to show the movies on. Our family definitely had a good time with those movies.

• he was the person who first introduced me to charity work. We both worked together for Habitat for Humanity. We participated in their "Blitz Build" and it was a great time filled with great people.

• he loved to take care of plants, mow the lawn, do yard work, and landscaping.

• of his ability to analyze things was one of his greatest strengths and one of his greatest weaknesses.

• when he and my Mom went out they never used to talk in the car. They just enjoyed each others' company.

• he would never answer the phone when he was home. He could be sitting right next to it, and he still would not answer it.

• of his ingenuity. I found a piece of paper for an idea he had written down for a pop-up tee for golfers. Ironically, my Dad only swung a golf club a handful of times in his life.

• when he got home from work every night it was obvious that he put 100% of himself into the job every day. The problem there was little that remained for home.

• he reworked the duct system in our basement so that we would get more efficient air flow through the bedrooms. He tried to explain it to me as I sat there with crossed eyes. I could not have been more confused.

• he was a parent for almost 50 years. He was a parent to his mother and father because of the language barrier when they came to this country. Then, he was a parent to his kids. It takes quite a person to do that.

* he was passionate about maintaining a good financial education. He worked on his computer until 2:00 AM and got up three hours later for work. I have found the discipline of a strong work ethic useful in my life too.
* he always seemed to brag about me to other people. I just never heard it from him and I rarely believed other people when they told me. My Mom's cousin told me after I read a poem at my Grandma's funeral that my Dad had tears in his eyes. I asked him, "Are you sure you have the right Dad?" I have no idea why he never told me. It will forever remain a mystery.
* he taught me how to make a milkshake. It was not just any milkshake, it was the best tasting milkshake you could make at home.
* he did some work before a big family party and then complained because nobody helped him.
* he never drank hard liquor in his life. If he had anything to drink, which wasn't very often, it was either beer or wine.
* he liked to be in charge of things. He figured that if he was in charge, not much could go wrong.
* he painted the den a light blue color. My Mom did not like it, so he had to repaint it and, to me, it still looks light blue.
* he designed the house we lived in during much of my childhood, and each of us got our own bedroom.
* the day before he died, he took my Mom and my aunt to visit my Mom's aunt who was not doing very well. Ironically, they both died within the same week.
* the smell of coffee in the morning reminds me that he always made it around 5:30 or 6:00 AM every morning.
* he always made it a habit to read and keep up on current events in his field. His briefcase was always stacked with articles and books about sales and engineering.
* one of my best friends and my Dad shared a mutual interest in fossils and rocks. My friend is an Earth Science teacher and my Dad collected rocks for years. Both of them knew I could have cared less. It was actually a joke between them. My Dad gave my friend a fossil once and he used it as a demonstration piece in his classroom. My friend sent him a thank you note and that was one of the few times my Dad ever called me on the phone to tell me that he had received this little note in the mail. He was very proud of that fact.

- at times he struggled with explaining and teaching people how to do things. He figured that it was much easier to do things himself.
- I cannot fix a broken doorknob when it falls off.
- he always knew how to cook my steak perfectly on the barbeque.
- he seemed to enjoy spending time with my friends when they came over.
- he could fix ANYTHING, and I can fix NOTHING.
- he believed that most of the time hard work had to be painful.
- he ALWAYS helped someone who was less fortunate than him.
- of his legendary work ethic.
- he truly enjoyed the challenges of starting and growing a business.
- he stressed the importance of our family eating dinner together every night.
- he took care of me after I had surgery in 1996.
- he had an insatiable curiosity about how things worked.
- he NEVER threw anything away.
- he took my Mom out on a date every week.
- he never really looked like he had much fun at a wedding.
- his work bench downstairs still looks like a tornado passed through there.
- the day before he died he updated all medical and financial records for our family. The printout was on his desk and outlined his retirement and budget from now through 2013. It was dated January 28, 2006. That really captures the essence of my Dad. He always knew where he was headed and he diligently prepared for the future.

CHAPTER 3
Advice

> *"It is one of the most beautiful compensations of this life that no man can sincerely try to help another without helping himself."*
>
> —*Ralph Waldo Emerson*

My Dad would laugh at this chapter if he was reading this book. He never thought I listened to him ever. But people listen in very different ways. My Dad always led by example, and he always tried to set the best example for those around him, especially his children. My Dad, over the years, had many wise words to say and he was always careful in choosing the action he would take. Well Dad, here is a big shock. I did listen, and closely, at times. Even YOU would be impressed. Listen to your Dad, though, because you never really know when he might say or do something that changes your life.

I miss my Dad because…

- one of the final lessons he taught us was to take care of yourself and never stop asking questions.
- his approach to every situation was very simple. First, get all the facts. Then analyze them. Finally, make an informed decision based on the facts that you have gathered.

✴ one of the coolest things he ever did for me was that he helped me achieve my goal of becoming a physical therapist. As with most health care professionals, you need to pass a licensing board exam in your state to be certified in your chosen field. I had a tough time passing the board exam. I failed it twice and when I was taking it for a third time my Dad interrupted my studying one night. He asked me, "Do you think you are going to pass?" I said, "Nobody ever gets lucky the fourth time they do something." He laughed. It was his way of showing me that he appreciated and respected my struggle to achieve a goal. My Dad checked the website every single day after I took the board exam for the third time. I was sleeping one Saturday morning and when I opened the door I ran into a bunch of papers that were taped together spanning the width of the door. When I picked the papers up, it was five pieces of paper taped together with my license number on it saying I had finally passed the board exam. Underneath the license number were the words, "GOOD JOB ERIC" written by Dad in his trademark capital letters. I passed by two points. I keep that printout with me to this day.

✴ when he showed confidence in me. I remember failing part of the ACT test in high school (see a common theme here?), it was the English part. I hated English. He turned to my Mom and said, "He didn't understand it." It was those unexpected votes of confidence that always meant the most in my life. And he was right. I did not understand it.

✴ sometimes when I would ask him what he was doing his response was, "Bug off." I found that humorous because the ornery side of his personality was taking center stage complete with the glint in his eye and those little horns protruding from his head.

✴ some of the best conversations we had were when I would call him at work. I knew then that I had his undivided attention and he gave me some of the best advice while at work and while in his "business mode."

✴ when he would tell us that money does not grow on trees. The message was simple: Value the dollar, respect the dollar, but do not be a slave to the dollar.

✴ he always used to say the phrase, "Give 'em hell" whenever I was doing something important. I think it was his way of saying "I love you" but that phrase used to annoy me to the point where I would cringe when he said it. Maybe I just did not understand the meaning behind it.

* as time marches on, they say that generations get better and we are more apt to not repeat past mistakes of previous generations. I hope to become a better Dad someday than my Dad was, but that is a huge challenge.

* he would give me advice on girls to date. I used to laugh and I asked him, "What do you know about dating? You married the first girl you dated." He laughed because he knew it was true. Then again, maybe he laughed because I answered my own question.

* he always knew the difference between right and wrong and was a good teacher in that respect.

* one time when I was in high school he told me he really wanted to be an anthropologist. It was a dream that always went unfulfilled. When I asked him why he did not follow his dream he told me that "anthropologists don't make money."

* he let my sisters and I make our own choices about our lives. He was willing to offer guidance but the tough decisions were left to us.

* one time I told him, "No matter what happens to me in life, the toughest job I will ever have is being your son." I think he took it as a compliment.

* he taught me that everything is useful. Old computers, worn shoes, torn hats, people. Everything has its proper place and time.

* he let me try my first sip of beer at age twelve. He said to me, "If you are going to try it, try it in front of me first." So I did. And then I said, "You drink it."

* he never dwelled on the past, always concentrated on the present, and looked forward to the future.

* he paid to help a child have an operation to restore his eyesight. The family was not going to be able to afford the operation so my Dad stepped in. I did not find out about it until after he died. But that was typical of him, he never broadcast the times when he did good things for people, he just did them. This singular act of kindness defined the type of person he was. Do good always and anonymously.

* he always was content where he was in life. He did not value material possessions at all and they never made him happy.

* he defined success on how good of a person you are not how much money you have.
* one of the worst things I could imagine now is to have a fractured relationship with him while he was alive. A couple of close friends are going through this very thing with their fathers and my heart genuinely goes out to them. Both sides need to be willing to compromise and want to genuinely make things work.
* the greatest compliment he ever gave me was that I was a good public speaker. He said that not only was I good but I was also a lot better than him. I had to have him repeat it, because I was unsure of what I heard. It was the only compliment I actually remember him paying me.
* he always said, "Eric, there is no such thing as a free lunch." Only years later did I finally figure out what he was talking about.
* he would always leave you thinking about the different options a set of circumstances presented you with. If not Plan A, then use Plan B.
* he used to tell me: "Everybody makes choices in life. Not making a choice at all is making a choice too."
* he always said that when I was growing up that I was "book smart and common sense stupid". Dad, I hate to disappoint you, but I was not all that smart with books either.
* he would yell at me for leaning back in chairs. He would always say "You're gonna fall." And I would say, "No I'm not." Then one time I really did fall and I started to laugh. He did not find it amusing.
* he told me there were two kinds of people in this world: excuse makers and difference makers. He said, "Don't be the first one."
* I used to laugh at him when he asked me who I was dating. He always said, "Eric, you should try that E-Harmony." I think he thought it was religious.
* I regret tuning him out at times when he probably was making some very relative points in an effort to "reach out." My stubbornness refused to listen to him.
* he NEVER cared if he was liked but ALWAYS cared if he was respected.
* he always rooted for the underdog. I think he saw himself in that same light. It was easier for him to relate to.

❋ I saw him eating blueberry pie once when I was real young. I told him that looked gross. He said, "You haven't even tried it." I eventually did and it still remains one of my favorites today.

❋ he is not here with us. They say you are 50% of each parent when you are born. Having had three kids, I would like to believe he left 150% of himself here. That was my Dad, the consummate overachiever.

❋ he always thought if we did not wear a coat outside we would get sick or catch a cold even though it rarely ever happened.

❋ he reminded us that somebody was starving somewhere in the world and would be glad to eat the food that we frowned upon.

❋ he taught us to respect other cultures. This was especially important since he was not born in the United States.

❋ as long as you would have a plan for things, whether it be vacuuming the floor or how much money you wanted to make in 20 years, you would have his support.

❋ he would much rather listen than talk. He always believed you learned more when you listened.

❋ when he asked how I wanted my hamburger cooked I used to tell him, "Brown." He said, "Brown is a color, well done is a temperature."

❋ he was the one who told me when I was in high school that I needed to be responsible for my financial future.

❋ most of the time he solicited very few, if any, opinions on decisions he made. Sometimes perceived as confidence, it was at other times considered closed-mindedness.

❋ he taught that it was a lot of hard work to run and maintain a proper business. It was not a 9-to-5 job and "anybody who thought it was, would not be in business very long."

❋ he took me into his office when I was 10. I told him, "Your office is kinda small." His reply was, "You don't need a big office to get work done."

❋ I sometimes blame myself for not convincing him that physical fitness was important. He usually blew it off and rarely took it seriously.

❋ he was uncomfortable receiving help from others. He never wanted to owe anybody anything. This is one thing I made sure NOT to adopt from him.

❋ at times, he handled my problems no matter how trivial they seemed to be. I remember once in 9th grade, I was angry that my friends were not eating lunch with me. I was just starting high school and apparently that was a big deal. My Dad said, "Go make some new friends and I am sure that your other friends will come back." I did. And they did.

❋ when we were growing up he always said, "One TV in the house is enough." If you were sick in bed, then you got the black-and-white TV moved into your room. Can you imagine that happening today?

❋ at times I got so frustrated trying to talk to him. As a result, my solution to the problem was not to talk to him, which was a pretty dumb solution to a problem.

❋ he taught me to never be satisfied with anything. I once asked him, "Even if I was the President of the United States, it still would not be good enough. You would think what other country could he be the President of?" He did not answer that question, validating my belief that he would never be satisfied with most things that I did. I think at that moment I also realized that as long as I was satisfied with what I was doing, that is truly what mattered. Today, never being satisfied remains one of my greatest strengths as well as one of my greatest weaknesses.

❋ had he lived I do not know if anything would have changed in our relationship. Then again, why would it? Would there be any good reason to change it?

❋ I thought he was the toughest person to live with. Nobody else seemed that difficult in comparison to him. I guess he expected to teach me patience and tolerance, two things that not enough people exhibit in today's world.

❋ he taught me that "nothing was impossible as long as you believed that it was not impossible."

❋ he always told me: "The people who are luckiest in this world are the people who die a quick and painless death." Ironically, he would consider himself to be one of those lucky people.

❋ even in death he taught us that true family and friends will always be with you for the triumphs and tragedies of your life. Those that are not deserve neither your time nor attention.

❋ there are signs that he is here. I tripped over his shoes in the garage going to my car as I was trying to hurry out of the house. His voice echoed in my mind: "One thing at a time."

❧ he truly understood the power of giving from the heart with no expectations of anything in return.

❧ never have two people approached a solution to a problem differently than my Dad and I.

❧ he legitimately asked for my advice as a physical therapist about a shoulder problem his friend was having. Afterwards, I could not believe he asked my opinion on the matter and actually listened to it.

❧ he never valued "book smarts" in an individual. He said that common sense was much more useful and important.

❧ he always said, "When I die, I just want to lay down near a mountain and that's it. Let nature take its course." Five months before his death, we were in the Grand Canyon. I have written on this pivotal point in our lives in a later chapter.

❧ he taught us the importance of making a decision and accepting the consequences of those decisions.

❧ he never liked it when we had friends stay over for the night. I remember him saying that "It is not my responsibility to look after other people's kids." I just wanted to hang out with my friends.

❧ my two sisters and I would ask him how his day was at work and he would always say, "Great." We always knew he was lying because he gave that same answer every day, in the same deep tone of his voice with a hint of insincerity, and then looked like he got the emotional and mental hell beat out of him.

❧ I stopped thinking about the differences we had, as there were many. I focused more on the similarities and the positive things between us and that has made a great difference.

❧ when he would try to teach me something, I would tune him out because I thought he was either misinformed or out of touch. I now know that I was the one who was misinformed and/or out of touch.

❧ he was the first person to teach me that not every person in this world is going to like you for who you are. He made sure, however, that I knew that accepting myself for who I was the most important lesson to learn.

❧ he taught me that being a good person is of the utmost importance. After that, he believed, everything else falls into place.

* he believed in the capacity for people to show respect and love towards each other. And if you could not do that, than you did not amount to much.
* he taught me that it is not fulfilling to work for someone else, and encouraged me to live my own dream.
* he taught me that "the reality of any situation is the most important thing in trying to understand the situation."
* he cautioned me, "You're a big dreamer, Eric." My response to him was simple: "Big dreams usually come true."
* he was good at accepting change. One of his favorite lines was, "You aren't going to change others, you can only change yourself."
* he was great at leaving the past in the past and he never held a grudge toward anybody.
* he believed that praise was a gift and criticism was where learning took place.
* he was such a great role model on how to be a good Dad.
* he was my greatest motivator, even though I never shared that with him.
* he told me, "The only person that can make you happy is yourself."
* he always kept things in proper perspective.
* of his perseverance towards succeeding in business.
* to him it was important to believe in something greater than all of us.
* it was important to have faith in each and everything that you do.
* of his ability to focus on the future and learn valuable lessons from the past.
* of his sense of responsibility toward mankind.
* he would always tell me, "there is a right way to do everything."
* he told me: "there is no such thing as bad luck. Everyone makes their own luck."
* of his unquestionable character.
* of his consistency to uphold his values at all times.
* he thought most of my ideas were nuts. It was fun proving him wrong sometimes.
* he looked for the good in most people.
* of his courage to try new things.
* he bought a new car only once in his life: for my Mom.

- he was true to himself and that is all you can really ask of another individual.
- he taught me that sometimes the best decision in life is NOT to do something.
- he instilled a strong sense of faith in me.
- one of his principles that he led his life by was: Do what is RIGHT. Always.
- he valued intelligence in everybody.
- he thought the world needed to be increasingly environmentally conscious.
- he taught us that putting others down is a sign of weakness within yourself.
- he believed more expensive did not necessarily equal more quality.
- he believed that everything happened for a reason.
- he did not tolerate stupidity from anybody, including himself.
- he always seemed to know the right thing to say at a funeral.
- he always taught me to lead by example. Actions speak much louder than words.
- when I become a Dad and have kids, I will not be able to turn to him for advice.
- he told me that, "One idea can make a difference."
- his passing ingrained in me the idea to live each moment in life to the absolute fullest and to truly appreciate each day for what it is: an opportunity to be the best you can be.

CHAPTER 4
Humor

> *"Make a man laugh a good hearty laugh, and you've paved the way for friendship. When a man laughs with you, he, to some extent, likes you."*
>
> —Dale Carnegie

I am convinced that the longer I live, the funnier people are. Even people you think are not funny, turn out to be funny because sometimes it is just good to laugh with people and appreciate the way that they are without any reservations. My Dad was no different.

It really took a special occasion for him to really laugh, and it was refreshing to see when he was in a genuine good mood. I thought my Dad was funny and I swore one day I would make that same plea to God that every kid makes; that I would not take after my Dad. Well, Dad, I have to tell you I DO think that I have a much better sense of humor than you. But then again, this is not entirely fair because you do not get to vote in this. Next to my Mom, he was the one that I spent the most time with since being introduced to this world. Here is some humor we shared and I encourage you to remember the funny moments with your Dad. These are the moments worth talking about.

I miss my Dad because…

* when he fell asleep in the living room and we would all laugh because his head would bob up and down like a fishing lure. At this point we are thinking he is going to dislocate his neck or is he really even breathing? The snores would start quiet and get louder and louder. Then, when he let out his biggest buzz-saw snore, he would wake up. We laughed hysterically because he would always wake himself up in this manner, but he swore it was because the TV was too loud most of the time. When he finally regained consciousness, he would look at us all and the first person he made eye contact with, he would say, "Real funny" in an agitated tone. He would get up, get something to drink, and make that "Ahhhh" sound after each sip. Then he would go get his briefcase and start doing stuff for work on the kitchen table. That happened about three to four nights a week for as long as I can remember.
* when he used to ask my sisters and I, "Do we have stock in Detroit Edison?" while referencing the fact that we wasted too much electricity by leaving lights on in the house.
* he never developed the ability to laugh at himself. It was not the kind of person he was.
* he took me to Home Depot with him. It was his favorite store. I would go one way and he would go the other trying to find what we were looking for. He never really told me what we were looking for, so I thought why not have some fun and explore the store? The problem was when he could not find me, his line was always the same: "Where the hell were you?" I always laughed when he said that.
* he attempted to explain to me how spark plugs worked in a car and I listened. It was a hot summer day and my Dad and I were together over the hood of the car. His teaching abilities were so good that day; in such, that I not only understood what he was telling me about spark plugs, but I also could repeat it back to him. My sister came out and took a picture of us together over the hood of that car because women seem to think that male bonding stuff is cute for some reason. It was truly a memorable experience because we had this synergistic thinking over spark plugs! It was the first time I realized that my Dad and I could be on the same page if we needed to be. I

was actually getting excited about spark plugs because this was a key to fix our sick car. After all the explanations and understanding about the anatomy of a spark plug, he went to go turn the car on, and it still did not start. But we had a great talk, and I remember that day like it was yesterday.

* he used to tell me, "money doesn't grow on trees." I replied, "it depends on the type of tree." He just rolled his eyes.

* he wore shirts from 20 years ago. Oddly enough, they came back into style. I guess there is something to this consistency idea.

* we both hate the sun. We tanned like candy canes, starting off white, burning a deep red, and finally returning to our milky-white tone.

* I remember going with him to the bank to open my first savings account when I was seven. It was 1982 and there was $100 in there. I did not make another deposit in that account for five years. I had accumulated $370.82 in interest. I looked at my Dad and said, "That's it? It's been five years." He looked at me and said, "Oh geez."

* sometimes conversations we have are better now. I actually get the answer I am looking for.

* every time I asked him about cars, he used to share the same story. "I used to have a blue corvette and then I had to sell it when you were born." So one day I said to him, "Look at your return on investment with me versus the car. I will always appreciate the fact that you had to sell the car, but a car depreciates as soon as you drive it off the lot." I will be yours forever. I don't think he ever bought that explanation.

* one time late at night I was watching TV and it was apparently too loud. He got my attention and, at the top of the stairs, he was standing in his underwear with a T-Shirt tucked neatly in. I was shocked. My Dad was always clothed, even at bedtime. He started telling me something, probably about the TV being too loud, but I cannot remember to this day what he said. Honestly, I was grossed out. I could not get that picture of him and his tucked-in underwear out of my head for a couple of days. I must have done whatever he said, because I sure did not want him coming down the stairs so I could get a closer look. Looking back on it now, though, I laugh because he was yelling at me in the middle of the night in his underwear! So the big

mystery is what kind of underwear was he wearing? They were of the classic brief look and to be honest with you thank God that is all I got was a brief look.

* he yelled at me for running over the lawn when I backed my car out of the driveway…that is, until I caught him doing the same thing.
* I never got to tell him the following story about my Grandma, his mom. My Grandma and I went out to lunch one day about ten years ago. I made the stupid mistake of trying to park my 1986 Pontiac Sunbird in between two large vans. I hit one of the parked vans. We parked the car and my Grandma walks over to where I nicked the car. She said, "No damage. Let's go eat." I started laughing hysterically. I would have loved to see his face on that one.
* I always teased him with bald jokes. When he got mad, I would tell him, "Relax, I will join you someday. I might as well get the jokes in now while I can."
* I told him that someday I was going to be a millionaire and he looked at me and said, "Don't do anything illegal."
* when we would call the house and he picked up the phone, he automatically said, "Let me get your mother." Sometimes, we wanted to talk to him too. You barely even got the hello out before the phone was passed.
* my Dad asked me one time if I had to give him a grade as a parent, what would it be? I gave him a "B+". He looked at me and said, "That's pretty good." I said, "Well none of us are in jail, dead, or on drugs, so you did something right."
* when I was ten, my Dad asked me to do some filing work and organization of papers for his company. I was shocked and thrilled that he trusted me with such a big task at the time. We went to Dairy Queen after and he asked what I wanted. I said, "The banana split. I did a lot of work."
* I thought it was funny when he would call me a smart ass. He would follow that with, "You must get that from your mother."
* of a time I got locked out of the house in college after partying with some friends. I had a few too many and I really needed to go to the bathroom, but I forgot my key to get into the house. I had to go so badly that it hurt and I started to sweat. I prayed that the front door was open, but my Dad had our house secured like Fort Knox, even in

the daytime. The front door was always locked so it did not surprise me when it was yet again locked and I had no key. I knew that if I knocked on the front door, my Dad would yell at me because I forgot my key, but quite honestly, I could not afford five minutes to discuss this with him at the front door because duty called. I figured if I was going to get yelled at, it was going to be on an empty bladder. So I did what any kid might do in that situation, and I peed in a bush by the front of the house. There were four evergreens in a row in the front of the house and one of them turned quite yellow in the middle and eventually died. I do not know if peeing on the bush had in role in its death, but I did not have the heart to ever tell my Dad what I did. He never could figure out why that bush died, but he was still mad that I did not have my key that night.

* he drove with the car seat so far back that he could have been driving from the back seat.

* he trusted me with one job when it came to getting ready for family parties….get bags of ice!

* it would have been funny to see him live in a condo. My Dad was a rule maker not a rule follower. I would have loved to seen him try to abide by condo restrictions on what he could and could not do.

* he tried to comb my hair like his when I was ten years old and I messed it up. I told him, "I have more hair to work with."

* when I made a poor decision he asked me, "Just because your friends do it, does that mean you have to do it too? If they jump off the Grand Canyon, would you do it too?" When we finally did get to cliff jump off the Grand Canyon in 2005, I told him that "none of my friends jumped off with me." He didn't get the joke.

* I remember washing the cars when we were younger and he used to yell at me for putting too much soap in the bucket. Even then, I thought that was ridiculous. Was there really a shortage of dish soap in the country that I was unaware of? One time I purposely filled the bucket with a massive amount of dish soap and it flowed down the driveway and into the street. Thank God we were on opposite sides of the car that day. I thought it was hilarious, but he had an entirely different opinion of the situation.

- he used to wear white tube socks up to his knees with shorts.
- I told him he overachieved by marrying my mom. And he agreed.
- he thought in three-dimensions. I think I got screwed up on at least two of those.
- he trimmed bushes like Edward Scissorhands.
- now there is one less guy in a family with a lot of women.

CHAPTER 5
Sports

"Failing to prepare is preparing to fail."
—John Wooden

Sports are such a huge part of my life. I think I played just about every sport in my lifetime and I am a huge fan of both college and professional sports. There is not a game on that I find uninteresting. In my opinion, sports truly mirrors our daily life and the struggles we go through, and the beauty of it is that there is always a resolution and a definite conclusion at the end of every athletic contest. My Dad, however, was not that big of a sports fan. He was disinterested at best. He thought people living and dying over a team was an example of having your priorities in the wrong order. However, Dad was present for all the first major sporting events I ever attended. Usually it was just him and I, but sometimes others tagged along too. There were also the moments when we were on the same team together as either coach and player or coach and coach. This provided for an interesting dynamic. I will never forget each and every experience we had and a lesson could be observed in every event.

I miss my Dad because…

* he went with me to buy my first jockstrap.
* he took me to my first major league baseball game in 1983 which also happened to be the first professional sporting event I witnessed live. It was the Detroit Tigers against the Texas Rangers. I fell asleep in the second inning and, to this day, cannot tell you who won, but what an exciting day that was for me.
* he took me fishing when I was nine years old. I cannot remember where we even went but I was very excited to go. We got up early on a Saturday morning and it felt as if we drove forever. When we finally got there, we sat at the edge of the dock. He showed me how to put the worm on the hook, cast the line, and of course, how to reel in the fish. I caught three fish that day and he caught one. I wanted to keep the fish because I wanted to show my Mom. We threw them back into the water. My Dad and I talked often about going fishing again but it never materialized.
* the first time I flew on a plane in my life was with him. We flew to Chicago to watch the Cubs, my favorite team. I told him he was not allowed to talk to me for the half hour plane ride because it would shake the plane too much and we would crash. I was 10. The Cubs lost 12-2 to the San Francisco Giants. The last time my Dad flew on a plane with me was to Las Vegas. Again, I told him he could not talk to me for the three-and-a-half-hour plane ride because it would shake the plane too much and we would crash. I was 30.
* on his 38th birthday he took me to see my very first NBA basketball game: The Detroit Pistons against the Portland Trail Blazers. The Pistons won that match up.
* he took me to my first college football game in 1986. The University of Michigan defeated Northwestern that day.
* he took me to my first NHL hockey game in 1986. The Detroit Red Wings lost to the Boston Bruins by the score of 8-2.
* he took me bowling when I was ten. I used a nine-pound ball at the time and I was convinced that I could use his sixteen-pound ball. That ball felt like I was bench pressing a machine at the time it was so heavy. I went up to the lane with that sixteen-pound ball, threw

it down with both hands, and got nine pins down. I looked at him and said, "That wasn't so hard."

* in 1987 my Dad took off work on a Wednesday afternoon to see the Tigers play the Minnesota Twins. The game started at 1:35 in the afternoon and we had tickets in the center field bleachers. I was excited because I thought these were the best seats! My Dad was convinced that there was not going to be a huge crowd there because it was a day game and during the week. Dad was wrong. The Tigers sold out that day and the old Tiger Stadium held close to 52,000 people. It was about 90 degrees outside and we saw my Mom's cousin in the bleachers. It was a fun day and extra special for me because he took the day off of work to be with me.

* he took me to my first college basketball game at Crisler Arena in Ann Arbor in 1988. I am a huge college basketball fan and I was excited. He got the tickets from somebody at work and I could have cared less that they were in the upper bowl of the arena. Michigan destroyed Purdue that day 104-68. It was a great game and my love for college basketball has been strong since that day.

* he watched my first track meet in high school. It was so important to me that he was there. I ran the mile and almost finished dead last. I sucked. But he watched me till the very end.

* he was the one who first taught me how to jump over hurdles both on and off the track.

* when I went to buy my first pair of track spikes to run in, he came with me and showed me his old spikes. They were light blue with yellow stripes. Those were some sharp looking spikes. It was one of the few things that we had in common.

* he hated wrestling. My Mom and he took me and my two sisters to Wrestlemania III at the Silverdome. There were 93,000 people that day at the Silverdome. It was an awesome experience watching Hulk Hogan body slam Andre the Giant.

* on the day of my twelfth birthday, he surprised me and took me to a Tigers baseball game. They played the California Angels. We were sitting in the right field bleachers and were two rows away from a foul ball. That still is the closest I have ever come to catching a foul ball. The Tigers won the game and it was a happy birthday for me.

* he took my family and I to see the Detroit Pistons against the

Boston Celtics. Now what was so special about this game was that the tickets were free for signing up for our local recreational basketball league. All of my friends and their families went with us. Basically, it was a big party in the upper deck of the Silverdome. Did I mention that they set a record for attendance that night? They had over 61,000 people watch the Pistons defeat the Celtics. I think that attendance record still stands today. My Dad did not have the best time, however, because he hated large crowds and standing in line, and he had to do plenty of both at that game. But he still took us.

* he coached my Cub Scout softball team when I was nine and I was a brat.

* he took me camping when I was nine. It was for the Cub Scouts and it was their 75th jamboree. It rained from the time we left Friday afternoon until Saturday early evening when we had to evacuate the campsite due to heavy rainstorms. It was raining so hard that I could have cared less about camping. The local news was covering the story about how we had to evacuate the campsite. It was a disaster. The highlight of the trip, though, was dry clothing and Dad took me to Burger King. It was the first time I finished a whole Whopper by myself.

* he helped me become a better sprinter when I was a junior in high school. It was one of the more memorable bonding experiences that we had.

* he was the only person who went to my cross-country races in high school. I was not a good runner and, one race he attended, I threw up throughout the whole thing. But he stayed till the end of the race.

* he was my assistant coach when I coached Little League Baseball in 1995. For once I was the boss and he had to listen to me. I told him before the season started that this was the way it had to be and if he could not handle it, then he should not become my assistant. He accepted the challenge and, to his credit, did remarkably well and was a great assistant. I remember one time we argued about a call on the field. We were in the 6th inning of a game that we were up by two runs. There were runners on second and third base with one out. I knew that the batter at the plate had a tendency to hit the ball toward left field. I moved my left fielder three steps toward the foul line from

where he was playing. My Dad thought that was way too close and told him to move back. I looked at my Dad and told him, "Dad, I am the coach." I motioned for our left fielder to move back towards the foul line. On the very next pitch, the batter hit it right to our left fielder. He did not even move to catch the ball. My Dad looked at me and I did not say anything. I was ready for the next play. I would like to think that was a moment where he found I could make important decisions when needed, and more importantly, a good decision.

* he was good in a crisis. When one of my players passed out during practice, we found out he was dehydrated. He was very calm. He assisted my player into the car while I phoned his mother to tell her we were taking him to the emergency room at the hospital. We got him to the hospital and they treated him appropriately and the situation turned out fine. I learned from that situation to take everything in stride and, in times of crisis, to be part of the solution and not part of the problem.

* he made me learn how to swim when I was young when I did not like swimming. Fortunately, I had no choice in the matter.

* we both shared a common bond in sports. We both ran hurdles for our high school track teams. He set a school record in 1966 for the 110m high hurdles and went on to compete in the state meet that year. I tried to do the same in 1993 and missed it by one-tenth of a second. To this day, it remains my greatest disappointment. Unfortunately, I never had the heart to ever tell him that.

* surprisingly enough he bought me usually anything I wanted during a sporting event we went to. I used to get the same exact thing then that I do now when I go to a game: a pretzel with lots of mustard and a hot dog with lots of ketchup. He used to say to me: "Is that all you want?" I said, "Yeah, it doesn't take much to make me happy."

* he always beat me when we had arm wrestling matches. It did not matter how good of shape I was in, he always beat me. My buddy and I were talking about this one day and he could never beat his Dad either. He wisely referred to this phemonenon as "Old Man Strength". For some reason, Dads rise to the challenge of their sons. After telling my Dad this, he laughed.

* we had great horseshoe competitions together at our family

picnic. One particular time, he gave me advice on how to throw a horseshoe. Using that advice, I overthrew the pit and hit the grill behind it.

❦ he loved model train sets. He always loved collecting train sets and putting them together. I remember he tried to get me interested in trains as a little kid and I had better things to do.

❦ he loved to collect stamps. He was an old-fashioned stamp collector. Some of the stamps he owned are pretty historic in nature.

❦ I could never win a sprint against him on the track. He had jets in his shoes and I had crazy glue.

❦ the first time I ever heard him use the word "fart," I laughed so hard that I farted. It was at a soccer game, and he was helping me with my shin guards, when I was ten years old.

❦ he taught me how to play Bocce ball.

❦ I would have liked to go fishing with him again.

❦ I remember using his baseball glove to play baseball with. It was a Wilson mitt with tan leather.

❦ I wish he wanted to attend more of my sporting events growing up.

❦ life with him was like having a coach constantly be on your butt before, during, and after the game.

❦ it is hard to look at his old baseball caps in the garage and not be reminded of the fact that you should probably be doing yard work of some kind or another.

❦ he criticized sporting events when we watched them together. Then he would get mad when I left the room because I did not want to listen to his commentary.

❦ he used to tell me that watching sports was a waste of time. I still disagree with him.

❦ we would never have walked in our local American Heart Association walk without his influence. Our family did our first heart walk in September 2006. It was my Mom, one of my sisters, my aunt, and some family friends. The weather, ironically enough, was exactly like the day he died; gray, wet, and cold. The most emotional part of the whole event is when they ask you to fill out who you are walking for and you pin it on your back, in honor of the deceased family member or friend. I pinned my Dad's name on my Mom's back. It was difficult, but with his strength, we accomplished another challenge.

* I had T-Shirts made when we participated in our local American Heart Association walk in September 2006. My cousin made the shirts for us and they were navy blue with a gray collar. In white, capital letters, it read, "TEAM TOMEI" on the front. On the back in the same capital letters, it read, "ARE YOU IN?"

CHAPTER 6
All Those Little Things

> *"I desire so to conduct the affairs of this administration that if at the end, when I come to lay down the reins of power, I have lost every other friend on earth, I shall at least have one friend left, and that friend shall be down inside of me."*
> —Abraham Lincoln

This chapter is devoted to fun facts and little anecdotes about my Dad that just do not seem to fit into any other category. It is a "grab bag" of facts, opinions, and information about what made our relationship so unique. Most people have fond memories-the little things-about what specifically makes their Dad, who he is. Insight into what kind of food he ate, what movies he liked, how he approached life, and his personal likes and dislikes are all ahead in this exciting and unique chapter.

I miss my Dad because…

- the first time we went to a restaurant, just him and I, I was eight. It was called the Rustler. I got French fries and they came with the skins on them. I looked at my Dad and said, "Somebody forgot to peel potatoes." I could not eat them, but he could.
- we were so different. I am an extrovert and he was an introvert. I am primarily laid back and he was primarily serious. I laugh often

and he only laughed at something really special. I enjoyed the fact that we were different at times and I do not think he did.

* he was a neat freak and I am a partial slob. It summed up our whole relationship: The odd couple.

* I think of how much he loved this country. When he came over from Italy in 1955, he loved this country so much that he surprisingly never visited Italy again. My Mom always tried to talk him into going back but he never wanted to. She said that she would go with him and my Mom is not one to hop on a plane to go somewhere. But he never really talked about going back that I can remember. The desire was not there for reasons that we will never know. I think that is why today I have no desire to visit Italy. I figured if Dad was not that excited about it, why should I be?

* I got pulled over by the police the second time I ever took his car out. I will tell you that most kids would probably be scared to death to tell their parents they got pulled over by the police, but I was pretty confident. We get pulled over and my three friends are freaking out. I remained remarkably calm. I thought we were going to get pulled over because a couple of my friends were screwing around in the back seat. When the cop came to the window, he asked for my license and registration. The officer walks back to his car to check to see if I have anything on my record and I just told myself to relax and try not to say anything that will give you a ticket. While I appeared calm and confident on the outside, my hands could have slid off the steering wheel they were so clammy. He finally asked me, "Do you know why I pulled you over?" I said, "Not really." He said, "Your license tabs are expired on your car." He asked who the car belonged to. I said, "My Dad." I told the officer politely that my Dad always thought that you could wait until your birthday, and his was at the end of February, to get them changed. The officer said, "No, you have to get them changed at the beginning of the month." I said, "I will definitely pass the information on to him." He did not give me a ticket, which I was thankful for and, in all honesty, I would have never known that anyway. My birthday falls on the first day of a month so I always have to get them changed at the beginning of the month! So I get home and my Dad and I are talking and I asked him, "When do you have to change the tabs on your license plate?" He said, "By your birthday." I said, "Oh,

because the cop who pulled me over tonight for expired registration tabs on the car said you had to do it at the beginning of the month." I will never forget the look on his face. He looked at me and then argued that was not the rule. I said, "I 'm pretty confident that's what he told me." He got them changed the next day, but I am not really sure if he ever believed me or the officer.

* he was such a great thinker. He thought in a way that was very hard for me to understand and comprehend.

* he truly loved my Mom and that was enough for him. He had very few friends, acquaintenances, or social circles. He had her and that was enough.

* we saw **The Passion of the Christ** together and he shed some tears. That was the only time I ever saw him cry in my entire life.

* he used to wear this white robe with a little black umbrella on it that was colored red, yellow, and green. I think it was the only robe he ever owned.

* he used to slurp his soup because it was too hot. It used to drive me nuts. Why don't you just wait until the soup cools a little bit?

* he could not spell well. He would ask me how to spell words as far back as the 3rd grade. I was a great speller. I always felt really smart when I could help him for a change.

* he still never understood how I got into that car accident in 1993. I explained this to him multiple times and he had a hard time understanding how I reacted quickly so I would not injure myself. After repeated attempts, I gave up and told him thankfully nothing happened except a big bill to get the car fixed. I rationalized to him that at least I was OK. He did not buy it.

* he left us too early but was lucky because he died the way he believed everyone should go: quick and painless.

* one of his favorite restaurants was Champps grill. He always got the patty melt and waffle fries.

* he started his own business without graduating from college. He was a successful businessman but I do not think for one minute that he was interested in grooming me to take over his company as many fathers like their sons to do. He knew that we had different interests but I believe an expectation was for me to follow in the entrepeneurial spirit and start something on my own. He always

asked me, "Do you want to open up a clinic?" or "We should open a restaurant." He planted the idea to be your own boss very early in our lives. America's best success stories are stories like my Dad and countless others who were not born in this country, but succeeded way beyond their wildest dreams.

* he valued loyalty as one of the most cherished characteristics that a person could have.
* he spoke about his deep respect for history and how lucky he was to witness some pretty amazing things in the course of his lifetime.
* when he traveled for business he used to take this huge gray suitcase, with a "T" right in the front made out of masking tape.
* he shares his birthday with one of the great leaders of this country: our first president, George Washington.
* his favorite candy bar was Snickers. I also love Snickers but I have not been able to eat one since he died.
* his favorite late night snack was peanuts and he had the peanut breath to prove it.
* he always appeared organized both personally and professionally in his own way, which was only understood by him.
* I do not remember a time where I hugged him in my entire life. It just was not part of our relationship, but I have come to accept that as a normal part of our relationship.
* I always looked forward to him going out of town on business for two reasons: First, my Mom would always take us out to dinner. Second, he would always bring my sisters and I something back from wherever he was.
* I know how proud he was to have all three of his kids graduate from college. It all started with him going to college thirty years earlier.
* the only reason we went on family vacations was because my Mom talked him into going. My Dad would have been completely content to stay at home and not go anywhere. I never recall a time where he enjoyed any vacation we went on.
* I never got the chance to ask him why he never wanted to return and visit Italy.
* he was never a patient in a hospital ever. He was born in a barn in Italy and died at home. How many people can honestly say that?
* he adjusted well to a new country when he was eight. In his

mind he officially became an adult that day. When I was eight, I was watching Scooby-Doo and collecting baseball cards.

❧ my Mom bought a different flavor of Doritos on one occasion and he threw them back in the bag because he was so grossed out.

❧ he called on me for help when he hurt his back doing yard work. He could not move, and he was yelling my name for help. It was a very weird feeling because you do not ever expect to be helping your parent. It never occurred to me that he would need my help ever. It was the first time our roles were reversed.

❧ anytime he was angry, a squiggly vein resembling a coiled snake rose on the right side of his forehead. You knew you were in trouble when you saw "the vein."

❧ of the way he danced with my Mom. Slow dances, never fast, meaningful and lasting.

❧ at times it was enormously frustrating to understand his perspective in dealing with problems because he already knew the solution and you were expected to know it as well.

❧ my Dad and Mom paid for my spring break trip in college. It was so generous and it was my parents way of saying, "We trust you. You're a good kid."

❧ he was great at moving me in and out of dorms, houses, and other residences.

❧ he knew how to pack a car trunk with more stuff better than anyone I have ever known.

❧ of all the amazing accomplishments he completed during his life. He had so many things to be thankful for. I really hope he took the time to smell the roses along the way.

❧ he grounded me for falling asleep at church when I was thirteen. The nap seemed worth it at that time was my explanation. He was not amused.

❧ the only thing I saw him cook were scrambled eggs with Italian sausage. The eggs were kind of brown and he cooked them too long.

❧ he enjoyed being around other families that had the same kind of closeness that our family did.

❧ of his unwavering devotion to attend mass every Sunday morning. The irony of that being he was getting ready for church when he died.

❋ he was so excited to finally buy "vacation property" just months before his death. It was always his dream to own property in Northern Michigan. In November 2005, on a Saturday afternoon, we drove two-and-a-half hours and my Dad and I each bought a lot in the same subdivision my sister and brother-in-law bought in. It is off of beautiful golf courses and nature preserves, peaceful and serene. A place where you can get away from everything, it fit my Dad perfectly. We were all around the corner from each other. I remember my Dad deciding between which of two lots to buy. He really was concerned how my Mom would like it. He was very happy on the way home because finally a dream was fulfilled. He enjoyed that feeling for two months before he passed.

❋ it's hard to watch shows like "Mad Money with Jim Cramer" and not think of him. It was one of his favorites.

❋ secretly I think he was excited that I learned Italian in high school. I don't know if I was all that excited, but I took it because I needed a foreign language requirement in high school.

❋ he bought me a new lunchbox when I was six. I had this awesome lunchbox with all of the NFL helmets on it. Half of the lunchbox was red and half was blue. It had a blue thermos with the NFL logo on it. I loved it. I broke it one day coming home from school and the lunchbox would not close. My Dad said, "I'll buy you a new one." I thought he meant that he would buy the same lunchbox. When my Dad came home, however, it was Sesame Street! It was all yellow and had Big Bird on it. I had to use it because I needed a lunchbox. I really felt like a big dork though, but at least he tried. Going from NFL helmets to Sesame Street was clearly a step down.

❋ he never got to take my Mom to Hawaii again. They went there on their honeymoon. For Christmas 2005, he promised her a trip to wherever she wanted to go. Unfortunately, it never happened.

❋ he always set a good example of the RIGHT way to do things even when we did not agree.

❋ it is sad for me that he will never get the chance to enjoy being with his grandchildren.

❋ I wonder what is he doing right now? Is he eating a sandwich, mowing a lawn, or visiting other deceased relatives?

❧ my belief in God is stronger now that he has gone. I guess that was his point all along.

❧ his death showed that many people were influenced by having known him. Isn't that what we all want? To be somebody significant to someone or a group of people?

❧ I think he would have liked to see a tornado really close up and tell everybody he experienced it.

❧ he was thinking about something every minute of every day. Sometimes you could tell when he was "in the zone."

❧ I realize how much different his life was than mine. I thank him for the wonderful opportunities he provided me.

❧ in his death I remember all the good things about him. I wish it would not have taken so long.

❧ he was proud of the fact that he got three kids through college and two through graduate school.

❧ he always carried a briefcase to work. The briefcase over the years changed, but the fact that he carried one every day, did not.

❧ he will never know the business he built for 20 years will live for generations to come.

❧ he used to cook hot dogs on the grill for our family. One time when I was ten, he burned the hot dogs black. I said that I would not eat them because they were dirty. Ironically, I love charred hot dogs today.

❧ I do not know where he is right now and I do not know where to go to find the answer.

❧ hopefully he is throwing a wild party that never ends wherever he is. But knowing my Dad, that probably is not happening.

❧ I tried to be like him. I think most sons try to be like their dads. But then I realized, I had to be more like me and less like him.

❧ of his ability to embrace the difficulties of life and turn them into something better.

❧ one time he got really mad at me when I was little so I hid in my sister's closet. I fell asleep for a couple of hours and then he was mad at me because he could not find me. I did not tell him where the exact hiding spot was. I would not win that round.

❧ when I see one of those blue, pink, and yellow sunsets in the sky, I wonder if he can see the same thing.

* he is meeting a lot of famous people where he is. I am sure he remains thoroughly unimpressed.
* he used to save maps from 40 years ago. Most of them did not even have major highways on them!
* simple questions such as: "What did you have for breakfast?" "Did you do anything interesting today?" "Is Mom mad at you?" can never be answered again.
* at times it seems like there is so much more to be said. Other times, we probably said too much.
* he always helped make my transition from home to college and from college to home seem effortless.
* I do not think he would ever want anyone to ever worry about him right now.
* I always could have seen him hosting one of those shows on TV explaining scientific principles on why things work the way they do.
* he never would tell me who he voted for in an election. He believed that his right to vote was personal and private.
* he believed that anything could be accomplished as long as you had the right team around you.
* at work he was a totally different person than he was at home. At work he was nice, personable, would listen to people's concerns. When he got home, I thought who the hell is this guy? Bring back work Dad.
* he could go a whole day without eating and still be tremendously productive. I honestly think that sometimes he thought eating was a waste of time.
* the whole experience of losing a parent is absolutely surreal. It is like you are watching your life unfold in front of you, but you are watching from a distance and there is not a darn thing you can do to control the situation. It is the ultimate feeling of helplessness.
* he always told us to "open the light" whenever we were reading or watching TV. His Dad said the same thing to him. I responded one time, "How do you want me to open it?" He did not find that very funny.
* he used to wear a red sweater with his initials "VVT" in white letters on the left side of the sweater.
* it is still an unbelievably huge adjustment for our family. We take things hour by hour now, rather than week by week.
* I thought I would be the one helping my Dad cope with the

death of his Dad. Instead, I helped my Grandpa cope with his son dying.

* when there is a leak in the roof, or the furnace goes out, or my car does not work right, I think of him.

* I hated going driving with him when I was learning how to drive. He was always so nervous in the car, and I honestly do not think that he was ready for me to drive when the time came.

* in 1999 he bought me the book Rich Dad, Poor Dad by Robert Kiyosaki. It has changed my life forever.

* sometimes we just did not have that much to talk about. I learned later on in life, that was OK.

* he always took care of our fish tank when we were growing up.

* he never needed an alarm clock to get up in the morning.

* he never walked around the house barefoot and yelled at us when we did.

* once in a great while I would make him laugh.

* he used to have chopped firewood in the backyard and we used to light the fireplace with that wood. It was always a treat when we were younger.

* he would never drive a car that had a bumper sticker on it.

* he insisted on using a computer that looked like it was made in the early 80's.

* when he drank a cold beer, which was maybe once a month, he really enjoyed it. I always enjoyed the times when we drank a beer together.

* we could never talk him into playing a video game. He found them a waste of time.

* he had a bad habit of asking the same question over and over when he did not understand something. I think he thought the answer would change, but it never did.

* I see his personality living within my youngest sister. It is pleasantly disturbing how much they act alike.

* I think in his heart that he thought his only son would be a little more like him.

* a small part of me was looking forward to helping him when he became an older man.

* he focused on the negative too often. As a result, I think I have become a more positive, optimistic person.

* I envied my friends' relationships with their Dads. Some had a buddy-buddy relationship. I was jealous because it never seemed that way with my Dad. But it was what it was. Looking back, though, I am glad for how it turned out because I do not know if I would be the same person today without the relationship we had. I also realize that it is not the kind of relationship I want to form with my own children.

* he was such a picky eater. He only liked certain foods and he did not want to change something once he liked a particular food.

* he enjoyed the peacefulness of a new day no matter what the weather was like.

* I could have ended up with a much worse Dad. But luckily, I did not. I ended up with one who did his job to the best of his ability. I am eternally grateful for this.

* he would never buy us an Atari video game system. They were very popular in the early to mid 1980's. So instead of Atari, he bought us the Odyssey video game system which was the stepbrother to Atari at the time. It was just like my Dad to go against the mainstream.

* he had a habit of turning on a movie in the middle of it and watching it to the end. He enjoyed trying to find out the beginning of the movie. It was a puzzle that needed to be solved.

* I realized our family lived paycheck to paycheck. It always seemed like we had so much more.

* the toughest part of him not being here is not having the chance to say goodbye.

* we would be so much different and yet so much the same if he were still here.

* he is not here. I am reminded that there is only one irreplaceable thing in life, the gift of time spent with someone you love.

* he would expect his family to carry on and build on the already great life we have been given.

* it is a time now for me to reflect on my own mortality as the unexpected patriarch.

* the already strong bond within our family has grown stronger. My Dad would have been happy to see this. Death can either tear a family apart or bring a family together in a way few events in life can.

* the future seems so uncertain. Your sense of stability and security is permanently altered.

* storm clouds evoke good memories of him. He always loved a good thunderstorm. He said the sound of the rain was peaceful.
* the toughest time of the day for my Mom is the time when he is supposed to come home from work.
* he thought that our society was slowly turning into a society that thinks that commercialism and materialism equals happiness. He could not have disagreed more. He believed that the focus of the family unit as a whole was deteriorating and that people put worth into things as opposed to relationships with others.
* I recently heard a story of a man who had four heart attacks and lived. Why did my Dad have to die after just one?
* there is not a day that goes by when I do not think about him at least 6-8 times.
* there was no closure for our family. That is one of the most painful things to live with.
* it is sad that he did not know it was the end. Then again, how many people really know when it is the end?
* you feel like an orphan when you lose a parent. Your whole perspective on reality changes forever.
* he randomly complained about things. I did not think I would ever miss that.
* going into his closet and looking at his clothes brings back both good and bad memories.
* it is tough for me to adjust to the crying that occurs when people talk about him.
* as the years go on, there are more people in our family that are not here and my Dad is now a part of that group.
* he made our relationship more challenging than it had to be at times. Most of the time I just wanted him to listen and understand.
* I always went to my Mom for things that needed permission from school. My Dad needed to know every last detail and it was a chore trying to explain things to his satisfaction.
* it frustrates me to think that people are given multiple chances in life and continue to waste them while my Dad was afforded only one opportunity.
* he ate things out of the refrigerator with green mold on them. He hated to waste any kind of food, even if it was bad.

* he always drank his coffee black. He could not stand anything too milky or creamy.
* finding some common ground that we could relate to each other on was the hardest thing in maintaining our relationship.
* I enjoyed trips to his office, the few times I made them. His office was always what I expected: small, organized, and with very few things on the walls.
* the adjustment period after a death seems like it never ends. It is an ongoing process and always takes you by surprise whether you are ready or not for the change that lies ahead.
* he had all of his kids business cards taped together on his desk at home.
* the day he died was truly the darkest hour of our family's life. The day was snowy, rainy, and gray. It looked like hell outside and we felt like hell on the inside.
* I think of how proud he would be that my Mom is as independent and self-sufficient as she is.
* it is unfortunate that he did not receive a warning sign first that he could be in danger.
* of the great stories we found out from his business partner. It is too bad that we did not hear these while he was alive nor did we ask about them.
* he did not have a tremendous amount of patience for most things. Enough to get by, but he could have used a lot more in certain situations.
* at his funeral there were people that he had not seen or talked to in twenty years. What a shame that it took twenty years to reconnect with those people and he could not even talk to them.
* he would goof around with my Mom and flick her chin, a thing that she did not find very funny.
* on one occasion he phoned me at college in my dorm room. He said he wanted to take me out to dinner. I proceeded to ask him three questions: "Who is dying?", "Are you and Mom getting a divorce?", and "Did Mom put you up to this?" He was laughing on the other end. The funny thing about going out to dinner was that I carried on most of the conversation. He would have been content eating quietly throughout the whole meal.

* the last image I have of him is lying in a casket resting peacefully. But that memory is not the memory that will endure.
* it is still hard for me to think of my Mom as a widow. I really do not like the word widow because that is only a small part of who she is and what she means to our family.
* it is comforting, although unfortunate, to talk to friends who have also lost loved ones.
* one of the biggest things I miss is knowing that he is available if you need him for anything.
* I do miss talking to him. I could always count on him giving me the other side of the story even if I did not like the other side of the story.
* I am reminded of the fact that every person's reaction to death is individual and should be exhibited without reservation or judgement.
* my Dad had a part of the tip of his left index finger cut off in a lawnmower accident before I was born. Ironically enough, I asked him while we were cutting the grass, what happened to his finger. He said, "A little accident." Since he was being secretive about the issue, I decided to go to Mom for the answer. She explained to me the story behind the missing tip, which basically came down to him catching his finger in the lawnmower somehow.
* he used to wear velcro tennis shoes outside. I used to think those shoes were not very cool but he did not care.
* the patients I take care of every day provided a welcome distraction when times were the toughest.
* he bought me my first subscription to Money magazine fifteen years ago. When I started rolling off prices of stocks and mutual funds he looked at my Mom and said, "I think I have created a monster." I laughed.
* he never liked where he was seated at a restaurant, no matter where it was. It was either too close to the bathroom, or the kitchen, or the sun was in his eyes, or the chair was not comfortable. It made for an interesting experience at times.
* he was such a decent human being.
* he always had cookies and coffee for breakfast.
* he ate walnuts with Italian bread.
* he was happy when I went off to college because it cut his grocery bill in half.

- of his absolute dislike for cereal. I never saw him eat a bowl of it.
- he gave us a great childhood when his childhood was not all that great.
- I never saw him with his shirt untucked or messy.
- he used to wear a pocket protector to put his pens and pencils in.
- I really wanted him to see me as a Dad someday.
- he was a great uncle. I am sure my two cousins would agree with this.
- he was so opinionated. But then again, which one of us is not?
- we both loved "Good and Plenty" candies.
- being my father's son, I always wonder how much of him I picked up.
- he was such a great provider for his family.
- he never once bought anything new for himself.
- he taught me to respect the elderly and other adults.
- there was always a RIGHT way to do everything.
- I feared him and that kept me out of trouble.
- he had to be a parent to both his kids and his parents.
- he did the best he could with any challenge life presented him.
- everything he did made you think.
- he kept in his heart the less fortunate.
- most of his good works were done anonymously.
- of his fierce loyalty towards people who meant the most to him.
- he put ketchup on his tacos.
- it is difficult to know that he is gone and will not come back.
- he was fiercely protective of his privacy.
- he loved Junior Mints. That was the first candy I ever saw him eat.
- even his sock drawers were organized. Thank God he never looked at mine.
- shirts from the 1970's still fit him.
- he was the only one who could start the barbeque grill.
- his favorite cake was Devil's Food cake with white icing in the middle.
- he provided the necessary structure that family success was built on.
- of his innate understanding of how most things worked.
- he never seemed afraid of anything.

I Miss My Dad…

- of his great attention to detail.
- HE was such a good son.
- he thought rocks were REALLY interesting.
- he used to write in all CAPITAL LETTERS.
- we both loved mint chocolate chip ice cream.
- he was a back seat driver.
- I always had to remind him of peoples' names. He was never good at that.
- I can now relate to my friends who miss their dads.
- he was a pillar of strength in times of crisis.
- it would have been interesting to see if age mellowed his personality.
- he was constantly cleaning and reorganizing the garage.
- he loved my brother-in-law like a second son.
- he tried so hard to be a good public speaker the few times he had to.
- of his excellent negotiation skills.
- he tolerated nothing less than excellence from himself and others always.
- he would never stop and ask for directions when he was lost.
- he felt his greatest accomplishment was his family.
- he never stopped trying to achieve his goals.
- he was a patriot of this country even though he was not born here.
- he truly appreciated opportunities to learn and grow as a human being.
- he had to eat bread with every meal.
- he hated shopping, and I agree with him.
- of the class and maturity he brought to every situation.
- he was a master at preparing to get things done.
- I still feel like he is here at times.
- other family members say how much they miss him.
- it was unfair that he was not given a second chance.
- I hope to be half as good a person as he was.
- he taught me the value of money.
- he left for work between 7-7:30 every morning.
- he was a great son-in-law.
- he taught me humility.

- of his relentless pursuit of personal and professional excellence.
- I wanted him to celebrate his 50th wedding anniversary.
- important family decisions will now be made without him.
- my Mom is sad without him and that makes me sad.
- I will miss him putzing around in the yard.
- one of his two front teeth was longer than the other.
- he always had a quiet, inner strength.
- he never gave up except when it was time to give up.
- our family still asks the question, "Why isn't he here?"
- he was genuinely concerned when I was sick.
- I always knew that he was in my corner even when I thought he was not.
- his favorite magazine was National Geographic.
- he wore out the outside of his shoes when he walked.
- he truly appreciated the serenity and peacefulness of nature.
- he taught me to always respect women.
- I used to joke about taking over his company when he retired.
- he did not want to owe anybody money for anything.
- I often think what the future holds for our family.
- I had 30 years with him. Some people are not even that fortunate.
- it was hard for him to accept when his guidance was no longer needed.
- it scares me to think that I might be like him in some ways.
- my Mom was such a good balance for him between work and family.
- almost every tool in his toolbox had rust on it.
- he would wear my old tennis shoes and hats to cut the grass.
- he could speak fluent Italian.
- it is hard for me to wear his shirts or a pair of his socks.
- he always wore shoes in the house.
- I hope someday he is proud of me.
- we will not have the chance to take any more vacations together.
- he always seemed to have a green thumb.
- I always borrowed socks from his drawer.
- he would rather listen to talk radio than music.
- my Mom was his best friend.

I Miss My Dad…

- he always yelled at me to eat more fruit and bread when I was growing up.
- he always took the garbage out on Monday morning.
- without him here, my decision making seems clearer and easier.
- it gets easier to talk about him being gone, but never easy.
- his shoes are still by the front door in the exact same spot the day he died.
- his last meal was a patty melt. He loved those.
- I do not plan to die from what he died from.
- he lived so simply, yet was so complex.
- he once ate a black olive sandwich and it really grossed me out.
- he never liked looking foolish in any situation.
- he used lots of black pepper on food that he ate.
- he was an avid reader.
- I cannot see his blue Chevy Lumina in the driveway anymore.
- I walk into the house and can see him working on the computer.
- he wore a straw farmer's hat while working in the yard.
- I feel guilty that I was not there when he died.
- he made us more aware of our health as a result of what has happened.
- unexplained expectations have been permanently lifted from my shoulders.
- my role in the family is so much different now.
- no one will start the grill like he can at our family picnics.
- it is important for YOU not to wait too long to tell your Dad how you feel.
- I hope my son or daughter is proud of me someday and that my Dad knows it.
- I still talk to him every day.
- I am proud to be his son.

CHAPTER 7
Knowing Him Today

"The art of acceptance is the art of making someone who has done you a small favor wish that he might have done you a greater one."

—Russell Lynes

It still at times feels like my Dad has gone on an "extended vacation." He will come back at some magical time and things will pick up just before he left us. As time marches on, every day that passes is a day that he is not here. That is the toughest thing to deal with on a daily basis. So many good things have happened in the past, it would have been interesting to see what the future held in our relationship. I know that he is still with us and he visits us in ways that cannot be explained at times. It is comforting, however, to know that he still watches over us and guides us through both the good and bad times of life. I hope that he continues to be a presence in our life, even though he is not physically here. To be honest I do not know if anything would have really changed in our relationship. There was no reason for it to change. The thing I am going to miss about the future is getting to know him as an adult, where we both can relate to common experiences that only parents and adult children can relate to. It is a time for reconnection with your parent on a different level, a level that unfortunately I will not ever experience with my Dad.

I miss my Dad because…

❋ oddly enough for as unprepared as our family was for his untimely death, I always felt strangely prepared. It was about 15 years ago that my Dad took a business trip to Colorado and on the day he was to fly back, a plane crashed coming in from Colorado. They had no idea where the plane was flying to or what airline the crash had occurred. The wave of emotions you experience in that moment of uncertainty is incredible. My Mom's initial reaction was to get upset, but after thinking with clearer heads and checking the flight schedule, it was obviously not his plane. But that moment gave me a glimpse into what the future could possibly hold. I always remembered that situation and stored it in my memory bank, just in case.

❋ my Dad always had a cross made of palms resting between two knobs on a cupboard in the kitchen right above the oven. During a family dinner, the cross inexplicably fell and landed on the ground. My sister came up with the classic line, "That was just Dad saying hi."

❋ at a family baptism nine months after his death my Mom, sister and I were sitting in the church. At the front of the altar, a burst of sunlight shone through the stained glass. It shined directly in my eyes to the point where I could not see. It then moved to my Mom who was standing right next to me. My sister and I looked up at her and she was just glowing in the sunlight. Her face and most of her body lit up. There were no other shadows from the light and the weirdest thing was that there was a couple standing in front of her and they were both 6 feet tall. My Mom is 5 feet 4 inches tall. My sister and I looked at each other and we did not have anything to say except to look at Mom glowing. That is how I knew it was my Dad. He lit her up and he nearly blinded me.

❋ since my Dad has died he visits us in mysterious ways. My Mom is a big fan of old pictures. Our house is full of old black-and-white photographs in old-fashioned frames. On one table in the family room, she has pictures of almost every family member when they were kids. She has her picture and my Dad's when they were kids right next to each other. Every so often my Dad's picture moves closer to my Mom's. I was over the house and once it had turned sideways so it was facing my Mom's picture! My sister and Mom swear that they have not moved any of the pictures. When I saw it with my own eyes, it gave me confidence to know that his spirit lives on in ways that are quite obvious.

* he was starting to accept me as an adult when he died. I think he thought all of those years of hard work teaching me the right ways to do things, in his mind, were finally starting to pay off. I was a good, functioning member of society and my Dad started to realize that. No matter what any son tells you, you always look for approval and acceptance from your Dad.

* it would be interesting to hear what he would say if he walked through the door tomorrow.

* he would have made a GREAT grandpa.

CHAPTER 8
A Vacation of a Lifetime

> "True contentment is the power of getting out of any situation all that there is in it."
>
> —Gilbert Keith Chesterton

This chapter deserves its own place for all the stories that happened in one week. Every time I would share a story about our trip, I was met with much laughter and amazement. It truly was an unbelievable trip. It is one of the few experiences in my life that I would not trade for anything. We took this trip from August 27, 2005 to September 2, 2005. We first flew into Las Vegas, Nevada, and stayed there for one night. Then we boarded a bus to a small airport where we flew on a small plane to a dude ranch in Arizona. We stayed at the dude ranch for one night. Next we took a helicopter to the bottom of the Grand Canyon where we stayed for three days and two nights. At the end of the canyon trip, we boarded a bus which took us back to our hotel and my Dad and I stayed in Las Vegas for an extra two nights before boarding a plane for home. This is the first vacation that my Dad and I ever took alone together, an entire week!

I think my family and friends were really interested to see how this soap opera would play out. How long would it take for Eric to piss off Dad? Would Dad leave Eric in Las Vegas, the dude ranch, or the bottom of the canyon? Will they fly home on the same plane together? Will they still be talking? Will there be two different recollections of what happened on the vacation? To find out the answer to these and other questions, this chapter will tell you all of the events that played out on that memorable trip, the last vacation my Dad ever went on.

There never was more excitement or anticipation for a vacation that I can remember than the trip my Dad and I took to the Grand Canyon and Las Vegas that last week of August in 2005. He had been talking for years about going on this trip and he knew darn well he was not going to get my Mom to go camping in the wilderness for two days without air conditioning and indoor plumbing. When my Mom suggested that he ask me to go, he did. I am not sure if I was option #1 or option #15 but the point is we went together and the crazy experiences we had in just one week filled a lifetime of memories.

It all started with the night before when he insisted on packing my suitcase for the trip. I did not have any objections to it either because I always forget things when packing for a trip anyway. I attempted to help him but he had both suitcases laid out on top of his bed and all the supplies on the bedroom floor. It was like a factory assembly set-up. Everything had its place and everything was put in a specific place inside the suitcase for reasons which I did not understand. I put some soap in the suitcase and my Dad gave me one of his classic, "What are you doing looks?" I knew then that it was time for me to leave the room and let him do what he does best, which apparently was packing for a trip.

Needless to say, I did not get much sleep the night before the trip. We had an early morning flight from Detroit to Las Vegas and I never sleep well before I have to fly somewhere. I just do not like flying, I have tried to like it and I am getting better at it, but I do not like it no matter the destination. My Dad, being the disciplined person he is, of course, went to bed right after the suitcase packing was done. When we planned this trip six months ago, it seemed like it was so far away. But here we are the night before, and I thought to myself in the middle of the night, "How in the hell are we going to spend a week together on vacation?"

My Mom dropped us off at the airport the next morning and that is when it hit me: vacation had begun. We were going to have to find a way to get along and have fun whether we wanted to or not. I thought of it as the ultimate father-son bonding experience. All throughout the years I heard of stories of how fathers and sons bonded through common interests. My Dad certainly did do these things with me, but not to the frequency which I would have liked. But I knew going on this trip, that HE wanted to go on this trip. His interest never waned as he was looking more excited about it than I was at the beginning.

My Dad was always so prepared for everything and this trip was no different. He went shopping, by himself, for most of our supplies for the trip. That is when I knew he meant business. My Dad did not go shopping for anything by himself without my Mom in tow. I was impressed. My Dad disliked shopping as much as I do, but he did not miss one item on the list. In fact, other people on our trip ended up borrowing some of our items. Be prepared, just like the Boy Scout motto says.

The plane flight going from Detroit to Las Vegas was nothing spectacular and I was very thankful for that. You want nothing spectacular to happen when your closer to Heaven than you ever have been. I was just praying that the plane would be half empty. My Dad absolutely hated crowds, and his comfort level was not great in these situations. We boarded the plane, and every time I board a plane I think the same thing, "If this is it, then it's been a good ride." Terrible thoughts for someone who is 95% of the time a positive person. To my disappointment, the plane was filled to capacity. I told my Dad I needed an aisle seat. When he asked me why, "I said if the plane goes down I can reach the parachute first, and be closest to the exit so I can jump out." Have you ever heard of anything more neurotic than that? My Dad just looked at me and laughed. I am sure he was thinking, "How are we related again?"

After the plane landed, we grabbed a cab from the Las Vegas airport to the hotel. The cab ride was not smooth and the driver got "lost" but I don't think my Dad was buying it. I was too in awe of Vegas to be paying attention to anything else, since it was my first time there. After the cab driver dropped us off at the hotel, my Dad must have forgotten to give the driver a tip, and the cab driver yelled sarcastically at my Dad, "Thanks for the tip." I asked my Dad, "You knew you weren't giving him a tip, didn't you?" He said, "People deserve tips for good service. We are too accepting of bad service in this country." Right on man. A few years ago, I would have been completely embarrassed at that, but at that point I totally agreed with him. Why should we pay for bad service? Then I realized, that I might be more like him than I thought.

After checking in the hotel, my Dad does what he always does right after we check into a hotel on vacation, fall asleep for 2 hours. I was not tired at all. I was wide awake watching a preseason NFL football game. When my Dad awoke from his little nap he asked me what I wanted to do. He said, "Are you hungry?" I told him that was a relative question: "I am always hungry." He said, "Let's go walk the strip and see if we can find something to eat." I thought this was going well.

Las Vegas is known for their buffets and I could eat just about anything. I wasn't really all that hungry because I was looking forward to our official trip starting tomorrow with a combination of nervousness and excitement. Then we walked that strip. And walked, and walked. We were at the far north end, and we walked past every single hotel imaginable. It was ridiculous. We were out there for three-and-a-half hours. There were so many people there and it was 108 degrees outside. He could tell I was getting a little frustrated so he asked me what was wrong. I said, "I'm hot, tired, crabby, and we haven't had dinner yet." My Dad could go for hours without eating, but not me. I finally told him, "I want a Gatorade, and then I want to go back to the hotel." I probably sounded like a five-year-old but at that point I really didn't care. That was the end of the strip walk and I was so tired from that, I fell asleep and did not eat dinner. I thought to myself, "this is not a good start."

We ate breakfast the next morning at the hotel and were both anxiously awaiting our bus to pick us up from the hotel and take us to a smaller airport just outside of Las Vegas. From there, we would fly to the dude ranch. Big planes freak me out enough, but small planes, are a different story. We arrived at the airport and it honestly looked like there was not enough of a landing strip for the plane to even take off. It was that small of a plane. I thought to myself, "Just be calm. Dad isn't freaking out, so you shouldn't either." But then again, he always was so calm about the bigger things in life. I swear

I had to go to the bathroom four times before we boarded that plane. The flight was delayed about two hours because of some "mechanical difficulties." I thought to myself, great, mechanical difficulties, which can mean anything from a wing falling off to and engine catching on fire. I got in and it was the first time I rode on a small plane with less than 20 people on it. I thought I would love the fact that the plane was smaller than most commercial airlines that people fly. Wrong again. I could not stand the fact that the inside of the plane was so small, I started to get claustrophobic. Of course, my Dad was right there to get a picture of me not liking this plane. I barely forced a smile for those pictures.

The inside of the plane was the size of a breadbox. It was ridiculously small. I thought to myself, "How am I going to do this?" Not to mention the fact that it was 100 degrees out, not that I already wasn't sweating enough. My Dad seemed perfectly at ease with it, and nothing seemed to faze him. The plane ride seemed like it was four hours long, when in reality, it took no more than 20 minutes across the canyon. I was looking forward to seeing the canyon, but I didn't necessarily want to be part of that canyon. When the plane finally landed at the strip on the dude ranch, I could not have been more greatful. I looked at my Dad and said, "Never again." He laughed.

The dude ranch was an interesting experience. It was very much what you would picture the old West to be like. There was the canyon surrounding you as far as the eye could see, parts of the ranch were dusty, and the ranch itself looked like a log cabin, complete with covered wagons in the back overlooking a picturesque mountain. Little did I know that those covered wagons were not only for decoration, but also options to sleep in.

We dropped our bags in a room at the ranch and the day's activities started. My Dad and I started with a hike up a mountain directly behind the ranch. It was during this hike that I discovered how much he cared about me. The mountain we were climbing was pretty steep. Being from the Midwest, you don't have the opportunity to climb mountains on a daily basis. My Dad told me to go up and down the mountain not side to side. Of course, I did not listen and went up part of the mountain sideways and slid down the mountain. I had a big gash on my right leg, to remember the event, and my Dad's comments about the matter would not be suitable for the average reader. I guess sliding down a mountain brings out the true feelings in people.

After a rest from my near-death experience, we got to experience shooting clay pigeons at the ranch. My Dad always talked with me about going to a shooting range near my house, and I never realized how much he enjoyed it until we were doing it. My Dad went first and each person got three shots at the clay pigeons. My Dad was the only one, out of approximately 25 people, who went three for three. He was right on the money. I was thinking to myself, thank God I never made him that angry over the course of my life. He had a great shot. I get up to shoot and my first shot fired before they had even released the pigeon. I badly missed the other two shots, but I was proud that my Dad was perfect.

As we were walking down some historical spots in the canyon the next day, one of the ranch hands stopped us and explained that said we could stand in the canyon and be in two different states at once: Arizona and Utah. I thought it was pretty funny because I hopped back and forth from state to state in the canyon. I yelled to my Dad, "I'm going to Utah, I'll be right back." He looked at me and rolled his eyes.

One of the best parts about the ranch was the homestyle feel to it. All of the workers treated us like guests in their home. All the meals were prepared from scratch and they even did the dishes by hand, which might seem odd to a lot of people who own a dishwasher. It was a truly a memorable experience, but I often wondered during the one day stay there if I could actually live at the ranch on a daily basis. I guess I am just too used to modern conveniences a thought to which my Dad would agree.

There was a period of time at the ranch, where I lost my Dad and I had no idea where he was, nor did anybody I asked. I finally found him sitting at the edge of a hill on the outskirts of the ranch taking pictures of the scenery. Then he was just standing there admiring all of the beautiful surroundings that go with being at the Grand Canyon. I must have watched him for about 20 minutes and it was truly a great experience watching him enjoy the moment. He seemed very much at peace on this vacation and enjoyed it immensely. It would be the last vacation he ever went on.

After a long day at the ranch, the sun went down and there was no electricity at the ranch at night. It was truly a place where you rose and slept by the sun. The sleeping options there could have posed some problems. Your options were as follows: you could either sleep outside underneath the stars in a sleeping bag or you could sleep in a covered wagon with two people facing each other. My Dad and I looked at each other and said, "We'll take the sleeping bags." Either would have been a new experience for me, but I preferred the stars and so did he. Mostly it was because we really did not want to be face to face while sleeping in a covered wagon together. A little weird. So, it was about 90 degrees outside and we were in sleeping bags! I was miserably hot that I think I got two hours of sleep all night, not to mention that I had Buzzy Buzzsaw next to me snoring the whole night.

My Dad wakes up in the morning refreshed, stretches, and asks me, "How did you sleep?"

I said, "Great. Just great. We're sleeping at least 100 feet away from each other next time."

"Why?" he asked?

"You snored the whole night."

"No I didn't."

"Continuing to be in denial about your snoring is not going to make the problem go away. When we get home, I'll ask Mom. Let's go see what's for breakfast," I said. The experience of sleeping under the stars was one to remember because I had time to count each individual star in the sky, since no sleeping was to be done.

In the middle of the night, I could not go to sleep not only because of my Dad's snoring but also because of me being uneasy about the helicopter ride the next day. The small plane ride went so well and I thought, how can I get out of this helicopter ride? I figured I might get a donkey and hike down the canyon myself, but the donkey was probably smarter than me and I can't navigate my way out of anything. So I just accepted the fact that I was going to get on that helicopter the next morning. I was so nervous, however, that I had to go to the bathroom often throughout the night. Now with no electricity at the ranch except for in the kitchen and the whole place operating on sunlight, I had to take a flashlight with me so I could find the bathroom. I walked into the shower at first. When I finally found the bathroom, I tried to do my business as best as possible while holding a flashlight at the same time to find the toilet paper. It was not easy, but I did eventually accomplish my goal of going to the bathroom in total darkness. It made me appreciate the simpler things in life, like going to the bathroom with the lights on.

The next morning I was so glad to be awake so that I did not have to listen to the snoring. It would be the first time I was riding on a helicopter. We were going from the ranch to the Grand Canyon. We were the last group to go and the helicopter only fits four people at a time. I thought what the hell, you only live once right? I thought I was going to absolutely hate it, but I loved it. The perspective you get about the vastness of our earth is absolutely amazing when you are looking down on it. As usual, I told my Dad no talking while we were in a moving aircraft for fear of it going down. He laughed. I think he saw me overcome some pretty big fears on this trip and I am so glad that he was the one who could witness these landmark achievements. In fact, it was one of the many highlights of the trip.

My Dad started the day with his normal morning routine which included shaving. He felt like he had to shave every single day we were on the trip. He shaved for two days in the Colorado River! I got up one morning and he was sitting on a rock, using some kind of mirror, the water from the river, and a razor to shave. It was unbelievable. Shaving was last on my list of priorities for the vacation. I thought to myself, "Who am I trying to impress?" But that was my Dad. Shaving made him feel refreshed so he did it every morning to start the day off, part of the discipline of a routine. And yes, it bothered him that I was not shaving. By the second night when we got back to Vegas, he pestered me so much about shaving that I finally gave in because I was tired of his commentary.

On our three-day stay in the Grand Canyon, it was typical for us to be white water rafting approximately four hours, take a break for lunch, raft for about four hours, and sightsee in the breaks between. By about 6:00 each night we would set up camp in some remote part of the canyon.

On our first full day of rafting, I wish everyone could have seen his expression when I told him in the middle of the trip that I had to go to the bathroom, again same business as before. He said, "Can't you hold it?" I looked at him and said, "Probably not." Thankfully, the raft stopped for lunch and we set up camp. I felt like a four-year-old asking one of the tour guides how exactly we did this in the middle of the canyon without running water to flush. She gave me a "bathroom kit:" a plastic bag, toilet paper, sanitary wipes, sanitizer and directions on how to appropriately go. I laughed at the tour guide and said, "Is there any other way to do this?" She said, "Nope." So I ventured out to find a nice, secluded spot in the 108 degree Grand Canyon where I could do my business in private.

    I walked for about five minutes and found a spot where no one in our campsite could see. My initial thought was, "This would be a hell of a place to die, squatting while doing your business in the middle of the Grand Canyon." I really did not have much time to think about that because, in the process of finishing the task, a second rafting expedition was coming the other way and got a beautiful view of what I was doing. There was no point in trying to hide it. I heard a couple of snickers and some loud laughter coming from the raft. When nature calls, though, you have no choice but to answer. The lesson that everyone should take out of this is simple: If you can perform one of life's more simple functions in front of complete strangers in the blazing heat, then you can do just about anything you put your mind to.

    When I went back to camp, my Dad must have put the sequence of events together because he asked me if I saw those rafters behind the rocks and I said, "No, what rafters?" I did not have the heart to tell him that the whole raft caught me with my pants down.

    That same day one of the most exciting things my Dad and I did while in the canyon was cliff jumping. I am not sure how far we were up, but it was far enough for me. My Dad jumped off first and I told him specifically to, "Let me know when you are going to jump so I can take a picture of you." Not ten minutes later, I see this guy take a running start, jump right off the cliff, and into the water below. Of course it was my Dad, and I am standing there with the camera and my mouth open. I told the group I was with, "Dad's just do not listen." They laughed. When it was my turn to jump, I went right up to the cliff and he yelled my name three times to get my attention. He wanted to take a picture of me before I jumped off the cliff. I had to stop, turn, wave to the camera, and then jump. I felt like I was five, but it was pretty funny when I think about it now.

    The second day of the trip, the best picture of our Grand

Canyon adventure was actually taken by someone on our raft. It was a picture of my Dad and I underneath a natural waterfall in the canyon. It soaked us both, we were dripping wet, but what a great picture, and a great memory I have. Right after taking that picture we got back in the raft, my Dad spotted a ram standing on a ledge in the canyon. To this day, I do not know how he saw this ram. It was behind some huge rocks and I had to stand up to see it. But Dad always had a keen eye for anything involving natural habitats. We watched this ram for nearly 10 minutes in silent contemplation. I thought it was the coolest thing. Anyone can go to a zoo and see all of the common animals, but we saw a ram. The horns were the coolest of all. He took about ten pictures of it.

When we were setting up camp for the second and final night, my Dad thought it was the greatest thing that the tour guides dressed up like waiters and waitresses while cooking and serving dinner. It was a very professional set up they had for being in the middle of the canyon. We had steak and fish, vegetables, and they even made a cake for dessert. My Dad, of course, got the camera out and started snapping pictures basically because he wanted to show my Mom the luxury accommodations we were getting in the canyon. After dinner that night, my Dad spent nearly a half-hour deciding where we might camp. It was ridiculous. At that point, I did not care where we camped, but he was trying to go for the coldest spot in the canyon. I told him, "Dad it is 100 degrees right now. Wherever we camp, trust me, it will feel like hell." When he finally settled on a campsite, he decided that it was not cool enough. He had me go and borrow a bucket from the tour guides and use the water to "cool the sand." This idea involved me making no fewer than 20 trips to the Colorado River, a five minute hike away, filling the bucket with water, and my Dad pouring the water over the hot sand to cool it off. This process went on for over an hour, with me making continued trips back to the river. After every bucket, I asked him, "Is this the last one?" I sounded like a little kid. My Dad said, "I'll tell you when the last bucket is." It seemed like forever, but I proceeded to fill all of the buckets to his satisfaction and it was still hot that night.

There was no electricity in the canyon so when the sun went down at night you either used a flashlight or you went to bed because it was so dark. That last night in the canyon, it was around 8:30 PM when my Dad and I started to go to sleep. But neither of us could because I was hot, sweaty, and irritable. We laid on things that resembled cots and he said to me, "So what do you want to talk about?" Talk about? I waited 30 years for you to finally ask me what's on my mind and you are picking now to do it? It is 100 degrees in the canyon, I am irritated, hot, and he finally wants to talk about stuff.

I said, "Are you kidding me?"

He said, "Yeah, what do you want to talk about?" Right after he finished that sentence, one of the two guys who were camping above us let out the loudest fart.

I looked my Dad and said, "Hey, did you hear that?" He looked at me and said, "Real funny." That was the end of our conversation.

The next morning when we got up, I glowed with a sense of accomplishment. I survived a white water rafting trip in the Grand Canyon and I was having a good time with my Dad while doing it. Not everyone was so lucky on our trip. There seemed to be a flu bug going around the group and people were vomiting uncontrollably while on the raft. Maybe it was the water. It was not a good situation. For the next three days, my Dad and I hypothesized why these people got sick and neither one of us knew what the real reason was. It made for some interesting topics of conversation. The perfect conclusion to our trip in the Grand Canyon was when the tour guides surprised us with candy bars. For me candy bars are not ordinarily a treat, but after spending two nights and three days in the canyon, it was. I immediately grabbed two Snickers bars. I tossed the candy bar to my Dad and he opened it and ate it without saying a word. It was a great moment. I felt like I finally knew something about him, that no one else would ever know. We had a connection, our own personal connection, over Snickers bars.

When we finally got off of the raft, we said good-bye to the tour guides and boarded a bus back to the hotel. The bus ride took us back to Las Vegas, and thus civilization, but it felt good to sit on that bus. We passed by Hoover Dam on the way back and I don't know what I was expecting out of it but I was not all that impressed. Maybe I was overly tired and could not appreciate the magnitude of its size for what it was worth, but my Dad loved it. You could tell. He showed that "engineer smile" whenever he was fascinated about the way something worked. He got out the camera and snapped pictures like a madman. The best part of this trip was when we checked into a new hotel on the Las Vegas strip. It was truly the most relaxing part of the vacation. We would spend two days in Las Vegas before boarding a plane back to Detroit. It never felt so good to shower in my life when we got back from the Grand Canyon and settled into our hotel room. I think I took a shower for a half an hour. After surviving the rapids and the canyon, it felt great.

When we went out on the town that night, he insisted on ironing my shirt. I honestly could have cared less if my shirt were ironed or not because we were on vacation. We argued a short while about it and then he ironed the shirt. I thought that if that makes his vacation a happy one, then so be it. I honestly was so tired that I did not have the energy to argue.

The last day in Las Vegas was a sad one for both of us. I was truly enjoying my time on vacation with my Dad to the point I was able to tolerate my Dad complaining about little things much more than I normally would. However, we were slowly beginning to get on each others' nerves as time went on throughout the day. When we got back to Las Vegas, he was perfectly content to nap in the hotel room and watch TV, whereas I did not want to sit in the hotel room at all. I thought we were in Las Vegas. Let's go explore. I finally told him that I was going to sit by the pool for a couple of hours. Anybody familiar with my intolerance to heat knows that I cannot tolerate it for very long, so for me to sit by the pool for two hours, I was pretty desperate. As it was, I was paranoid about getting sunburned so I kept putting suntan lotion on myself every 20 minutes. In other words, it was not all that relaxing.

After both the pool and my Dad's nap we walked the Las Vegas strip for what seemed like the fourth time in as many days. He proudly showed me the hotel that he and my Mom stayed at 35 years ago, and he had the pictures to prove it. I remember him making me stand by this clown sculpture in front of the hotel. I told him, "I hate clowns." He said, "Stand by the clown, you clown." When we went into one of the hotels, my Dad said, "Your mother would love this hotel." We then checked out hotel rates, specials, the amenities, and took our own little tour. I think that my Mom would be shocked at how much Las Vegas has changed since the last time she went.

Neither my Dad or I are gamblers, and even if we were, we did not have the heart to gamble knowing that Hurricane Katrina had recently struck New Orleans. It just did not seem right to gamble away money when people were in need. Since we were not of the gambling mind, I thought why not go see one of the shows that Las Vegas was known for? Early in the afternoon, I went and bought the tickets and planned on buying the cheapest tickets at $65 each. My Dad came over from the opposite end of the casino and said, "If we are going to see a show, we are buying the best seats we can." My jaw dropped. I would have never expected him to say anything like that, but maybe it was because I was paying for the tickets. The new tickets were $30 more. We ended up sitting about nine rows out from the stage. They were great seats. My Dad noticed directly behind us there was a family of five; a Dad, Mom, and their three kids. The three children were all under the age of seven and the show that we were seeing was definitely not suited for young children. My Dad took the opportunity to tell these complete strangers just that. After he finished talking for about five minutes, he realized that the family spoke no English. Laughing hysterically, I said, "Don't worry, Dad, I understood every word you said and I completely agree."

He looked at me and said nothing.

I said, "Why don't we just enjoy the show?"

Twenty minutes later, he fell asleep! I nudged him and said, "Enjoy the nap? I paid $95 per ticket for this show. Could you stay awake?" I felt like the roles were reversed and I was starting to sound like the parent. After all of that, though, he did eventually enjoy the show.

For dinner that night, my Dad has never been a big eater, but he insisted we go to this New York-style deli in one of the hotels on our last night in Las Vegas. They had deli sandwiches as big as your head and as high as a small skyscraper. He asked me if I wanted fries with my sandwich and I said, "No." He then ordered fries for us. He ordered a corned beef sandwich and I ordered a Turkey Reuben. I finished my sandwich and he left half of his. All he could repeat throughout the entire meal was, "What a waste of food." Annoyed at this point, I asked him,

"Why did we come to this restaurant if you knew you weren't going to finish your food?"

He said, "I'm glad to see that wasting food bothers you so much." It seemed there was always a lesson to be learned, even on vacation.

On our last morning in Las Vegas he got up at 6:00AM to take pictures of Las Vegas as it was waking up. He asked me if I wanted to go and I said, "No." He must have taken about 50 pictures and his reason for doing so was to show my Mom and talk her into taking a trip there someday. By this time, we both acknowledged that we were officially getting on each others' nerves. The next big decision was breakfast. My Dad could not decide on where he wanted to go for breakfast. I suggested this breakfast buffet place in the hotel. He loved that place two days ago when we ate at it, but he did not want to go back there for some reason. So we wandered around for about 30 minutes until we decided on a donut stand where he bought two donuts. He asked me what I wanted and I said, "Not donuts." I did not eat breakfast that morning.

We sat in relative silence on the cab ride to the airport. We both loved the vacation but were excited to be able to see and talk to someone else. On the plane ride home, we sat with a seat between us on the plane. He had the window seat, which he loves, and I had the aisle seat, which I love. My thought is that in case the plane is crashing, then I can be the first one out with a parachute. After a week together, though, we both realized that we had done enough bonding for the time being, but continued to have a great time.

When we were on the plane together, I told him, "Thanks for the trip. I had a good time." He said, "Your welcome." That was the definitive conclusion of the trip. No frills attached. That was simply my Dad and there will never be anyone else like him.

Come to find out, he filled about three to four disposable cameras worth of pictures on our trip. He was taking pictures every single day. Some days, I don't even know where he pulled a camera out of. He always had one handy. He took pictures of EVERYTHING! Little did I know that he was planning to create his own picture book of our time together on vacation. The book brings back great memories as an experience in which only him and I shared. That vacation will never leave my mind and my heart for it was truly an experience where I got to know my Dad again. That book is still difficult to look at.

CONCLUSION

Thank you for reading this book. I hope you enjoyed our journey together. I know for some you it may bring back both good and bad memories. Cherish those memories because, in the end, that is really what we have. At times I hope you laughed and related to moments well spent with your Dad. I am sure that it felt good to cry, too, remembering those things that make a lifetime so worthwhile. WE are all in this together. No one is ever alone in dealing with the loss of a father or other loved one, and there are always people who have not told their story yet. I hope this book encourages them to do so.

More importantly, I wanted you to know about my Dad and the direct and indirect influence he had on my life. He was truly an amazing individual for the simple fact that no one can or ever will be exactly like him. Every relationship is complicated in some way. My relationship with my Dad was no different. The good times were really good and the bad times, on reflection, were not actually all that bad. Thank God for the gift of perspective. The death of a loved one can define you in one of two ways: it can eat you alive and consume all of your thoughts or you can find the positive, silver lining behind the clouds.

If your Dad has passed on, remember the cherished moments you shared together. Those moments will get you through another day. Equally important is to forget the bad times. In other words, the past is exactly that. Leave it there. Life is too short to always focus on the negative. Forgive your Dad for any wrongs you may have perceived against you, and, if possible, give him the benefit of the doubt that he truly tried to do the best job he could.

If your Dad is still alive, remember that you do not know when the race will end. Do not take for granted this fact. Make sure everyone celebrates at the finish line instead of wondering what happened during the race. My hope for all of you is that everyone takes time to appreciate their own relationship with their Dad or other loved one for what it is. If it is great, make it greater. If it is good, make it great. If it is bad, make it good. If the relationship is non-existent, then do not wait for that to become the legacy you both leave. The relationship you have with your Dad is unlike any other that you will have during your lifetime. Make it great, because you only get one chance. When that chance is up, let happiness follow at the recollection of time well spent. Thank you for your time and I hope each and every person reading this has found some value and application for their own lives.

> *"If one advances confidently in the direction of his dreams and endeavors to live the life which he has imagined, he will meet with a success unexpected in common hours."*
> **—Henry David Thoreau**

ACKNOWLEDGEMENTS

A special thank you goes out to my wonderful family and friends. Your support and encouragement through this process means more to me than you will ever know. Thank you all for being in my corner, now and forever. I am truly honored to have each and every one of you in my lives. Team Tomei will always be good and strong and we will live to enjoy many days filled with happiness and opportunity that our great lives provide us.

Since my Dad died I have realized that you truly enter adulthood when you lose a parent or become one. Thanks Dad for teaching and preparing this final lesson for me. Thank you for giving me a life to make all of my dreams come true. You're the greatest, and I know someday we will meet again.